Book of Daily Communion

book of daily communion

*spring forth with scriptures
journey with
the father, son & holy spirit*

KYRRA S D

PARTRIDGE

Print information available on the last page.

To order additional copies of this book, contact
Toll Free 800 101 2657 (Singapore)
Toll Free 1 800 81 7340 (Malaysia)
orders.singapore@partridgepublishing.com

www.partridgepublishing.com/singapore

Contents

Introduction xi

Preface xiii

Author's works & thoughts xv

Our Covenant with God 1

Our Lord & Our Saviour 11

Jesus Christ Our Saviour 16

Christ Jesus begins his Ministry 29

Daily Communion 48

I am a child of an Almighty God 64

The world is Peripheral to the Church 81

Our Saving Grace 83

The Revival of Humanity 84

About the Book 87

About the Author 89

Jesus
a revival through a communion
of declaration & prayers,
may the angels descend upon the shepherds
to send forth comforters

Romans 15:13 esv
May the God of hope fill you with all joy
and peace in believing,
so that by the power of the Holy Spirit you
may abound in hope.

dedicated to you ...

his beloved, his precious child,
in need of his Miracle!

Mark 4:11-12 niv

He told them, "The secret of kingdom of God has
been given to you. But to those on the outside,
everything is said in parables so that ...
They may be ever seeing but never perceiving,
and ever hearing but never understanding;
Otherwise they might turn and be forgiven!"

Introduction

Luke 9:13-15 *niv*
He replied, "You give them something to eat."
They answered, "We have only five loaves of bread
and two fish, unless we go and buy food for all this crowd."
About five thousand men were there.
But he said to his disciples,
"Have them sit down in groups of about fifty each."
The disciples did so, and everyone sat down.

five loaves & two fish
Here are our five loaves & two fish
May our hearts, souls & lives daily receive the
supernatural goodness of the Lord.
The goodness of the Bread of Life &
the fountain of Living Waters
Brought forth by the One Son of a Living God
Who descended from heaven, in exchange of his life to
free mankind & to lead us to the Gift of Miracles
His name is Christ Jesus

spring forth & multiply ...

Luke 9:16-17 *niv*
Taking the five loaves and the two
fish and looking up to heaven,
he gave thanks and broke them.

Then he gave them to the disciples
to distribute to the people.
They all ate and were satisfied,
and the disciples picked up twelve
basketfuls of broken pieces
that were left over.

Preface

in god we trust ...

Isaiah 55:8-9 nkjv
"For My thoughts are not your thoughts,
Nor are your ways My ways,"
says the LORD.
"For as the heavens are higher than the earth,
So are My ways higher than your ways,
And My thoughts than your thoughts.

Psalm 119:105 nkjv
Your word is a lamp to my feet
And a light to my path.

our rainbow connection ...

Proverbs 3:5-6 *njkv*
Trust in the LORD *with all your heart,*
And lean not on your own understanding;
In all your ways acknowledge Him,
And He shall direct your paths.

Genesis 9:13-16 *niv*
I have set my rainbow in the clouds, and it will be the sign of the covenant between me and the earth. Whenever I bring clouds over the earth and the rainbow appears in the clouds, I will remember my covenant between me and you and all living creatures of every kind. Never again will the waters become a flood to destroy all life. Whenever the rainbow appears in the clouds, I will see it and remember the everlasting covenant between God and all living creatures of every kind on the earth."

Author's works & thoughts ...

Thus I begin with hope for a celestial miracle, that this book be a catalyst and life changing to some stranger, whom is much loved. His beloved!

Dear stranger, I may never get to meet you. Nevertheless, I pray that this work finds you at the most desirable moment and manifests as a promise of a miracle. The long forgotten promise of a Heavenly Father, who longs for your reunion with him in a covenant.

In essence, here is my objet d'art, exhibited with passion, excitement and is the result of many conversations with my Heavenly Father, often held in secrecy, during such stormy days & nights. In fact, based on supernatural events that mystically led me to submit these artistic impressions from the age old, timeless Bible, to the publisher, instead of a poetry anthology.

God works in mysterious ways!

My initial intention was to consequently leave the selected scriptures, within a concept presented in an artistic manner, without any briefing of the author's work. As I would have preferred my innermost conceptual thoughts to be within my secret, sacred space. Like the Mercy Seed that's hidden in the depths of the Tabernacle. Where one approaches God in his holiness and in his righteousness, and we without sin, according to the Traditional Law of Covenant.

Nevertheless, the publishers insisted that there should be both illustrations & descriptions. As a result, leaving me to begin my covenant with the reader, sharing my deepest thoughts and secrets, profoundly painted throughout this precious book. I sincerely hope you enjoy the specially selected scriptures, that have been the ancient foundation and cornerstone of many civilizations. These eternal scriptures wrapped around my conceptual ideas, are as a matter of fact, strategically placed to encourage the readers to further reacquaint themselves with the Bible and appreciate its meaningful purpose and its timelessness. Such that this art form; monumental in a meaningful manner, simultaneously establishes the Covenant of Grace with a holy and living God. A relationship that is founded within the Trinity, as well as strengthened daily in communion. Although, earlier I was happy to leave the portrait in an exhibit and walk away, such purposefully leave an impression to evoke the reader's insights. As rightfully it should be...

Less of me and More of Christ Jesus.

Book of Daily Communion, is a personal initiation, as a fund raising idea for my daughter and a few of her dearest friends, graduating from their Bible College. A reason in similar to that they might guide a lost ship at sea, as it struggles within the unfamiliar charters of the ocean in the mist of darkness, while its crew prays for directions and a miracle. Therefore, let such a proposed church community be the lighthouse that unveils the adoration of God's love through his son Christ Jesus, the miracle that directs the path of many strangers toward the comfort of a familiar home. On account of a fact that I was not born into a Christian community. It dawned on me one day, that one should view it from a perspective of a covenant. Seemingly, at first I had the right concept of the covenant but the wrong approach. My former idea was that of a perpetual angry God, who waits around the corner to entrap us in Acts of Sins, as matter of law within the yardstick of Moses's Ten Commandments. However, everything has changed now and I have experienced God's love for me through the Covenant of Grace and within a Trinity. Presumably, as at that time I was not ready for I did not have the prolific knowledge of the Bible. I preferred reading articulated religious works of amazing scholars that shaped my thoughts, for that was certainly an accomplishment, but it helped me only to a certain extend. There was no authentic wholesomeness or steadfast transformation.

In the perspective of a truth, as the late Alexander Pope quoted, "Little knowledge is a dangerous thing."

Then, one beautiful Canadian Summer day, in June 2011, my daughter invited me to a church that she attended. I vividly remember walking for at least half an hour in search of the church. Here is one of my favourite quote by Lewis Carroll in Alice in Wonderland that complements my situation in good humour.

Alice: Would you tell me please, which way I ought to go from here?

Cat: That depends on where you want to go.

Alice: I don't much care where.

Cat: Then it doesn't matter which way you go.

Alice: So long as I get somewhere.

Cat: Oh, you are sure to do that, if you only walk long enough.

My life has been a long, exhausting turmoil of a journey. In certainty, here is my milestone and since then, I have nothing else more than to Praise Jesus! Eventually, I found the contemporary church within the premises of an old forgotten theatre. As a matter of fact, to place it more appropriately, Christ Jesus rescued me and all in his good time! That was my life changing moment. That was the beginning of a new momentous journey that brought me towards the presence of Christ Jesus. Then onwards, without doubt, I knew I was found for good and the resolute transformation began.

The whole service was an experience of absolute joyousness! The congregation with its heartfelt welcome, the encouraging and energetic worship songs, most of all a distinct atmosphere, fairy dusted with love. I felt the spiritual presence but couldn't explain my innermost consciousness. The presence of an enchanted community gathered within a celebration of a personified love. I cried silently during the service, for I must have felt the love of Christ Jesus. They were strangers, despite that somehow it felt like a familiar home. I had a heart transformation and felt a genuine connection of an instant informality that I couldn't explain. Before the end of that month, I was writing worship songs of Jesus. Precisely, that's what love does, true spiritual love, for it leaves no inhibition and no separation of individuality. There was no alcohol involved and the only good spirit there, was the presence was of the Holy Ghost. In essence of a clarity, my purpose in life made perfect sense, and I started believing in my worthiness, within the dimension of a universe, from a perspective of a much cherished celestial man who died 2000 years ago.

His name is Christ Jesus and through his lineage of his perfect love, unconditional in light of his sufferance at the cross, I am set free. Yes, now I am able to release my preconditioned inhibitions of who I was and moreover, that enables me to rejoice and embrace my new identity in Christ. This state of righteousness allows me to break free from an undermined perspective of my previous worthiness as it changes immediately. Furthermore, I have a brand new Covenant of Grace with the same God, of whom earlier I believed, that I could only approach in perfection. Yes, now, I am a blameless daughter of my creator.

The Almighty King who created heaven & earth has anointed me in a covenant as his Princess Daughter and bestowed me with full rights to receive favours and grace from him. A covenant based on love, pure spiritual & supernatural love. The kind of love that would move mountains for me. For now, with that well founded covenant, I could daily have an authentic relationship in communion with him. A long awaited and forgotten privilege regained in righteousness and received freely by the unconditional love of his son Christ Jesus. Our saviour, who descended earth and made it possible, so that I could be reunited in acquiescent to the love of a Heavenly Father!

Thus here I present the manifestation of my purpose within a miracle …. with much love,

book of daily communion

spring forth with scriptures
journey with
the father, son & holy spirit.

book of daily communion
spring forth with scriptures
journey with the father, son & holy spirit.

Our Covenant with God ...

Jeremiah 29:11-13 niv
For I know the plans I have for you," declares the LORD, *"plans to prosper you and not to harm you, plans to give you hope and a future. Then you will call on me and come and pray to me, and I will listen to you. You will seek me and find me when you seek me with all your heart...*

When you seek me
     with all your heart ...

Psalms 9:10 niv
Those who know your name trust in you,
for you, LORD,
have never forsaken those who seek you.

Our Covenant with God

In a diversified world, how do we explain God, not to mention our covenant with him? Within a balance, most of us know that God exists. I shall not address any stubborn atheist friends or family out there, all things considered, in believe of a saying "When the student is ready, the teacher appears." Nevertheless, as much as we live in an unpredictable universe, there is never a place or a moment that does not allow you to reach out to him. Seek Christ Jesus with all your heart and soul; never give up and expect miracles.

The Pastor of the local church that I attend, gives us the insight of the magnificent love of Jesus. In the light of Mathew 18:12-14 we learn of The Parable of the Lost Sheep. Jesus has the heart of that same shepherd, who leaves his ninety-nine sheep, in search of that one that needs rescue. The shepherd carries the sheep home and thus Jesus needs our permission to carry us through his will and to consciously work his ways into us. I believe this allows him to untangle the webs that had been pre-conditioned within us, as he restores us.

The poignant revelation of why we need such a restoration confirms the fact that we live in an almost unsympathetic world. A world that conceptualizes love as a celebration within its commercialized worth, thus badly failing the real test of compassion. Very seldom we experience the love that passes all tests and lasts till the end of time.

Furthermore, we live within the boundaries of a society of the self-made man. When such a man loses the support of his fallacious foundation and simultaneously loses control of his accumulated material world, formidably it gives life to the term. "All hell breaks loose!" The matter of the truth is by taking away both such indispensable pivotal support from him, within the confinement of a society, completely messes him up. Unless, he has a supernatural covenant with a Superior, Living God. A God whom is reaching out to us in the way of a Trinity, the Father, Son & the Holy Spirit.

We have seen and read too many of those heart breaking situations. A great example would be Wall Street, its victims and the number of suicide cases every year. Therefore, we need Christ Jesus, with his supernatural ways, the exemplary indispensable cornerstone, to help us build a rock hard foundation. We need to empower ourselves with his promises of the scriptures to work miracles right from the beginning of any life situation. Whether within the area of our finances, marriages, relationships or health matters, for the reason I strongly believe that the Christ holds the key that opens all the right doors and closes the wrong ones.

Having said that, everyone is entitled to their version of who God is, neither will I undermine the ingenuity of God's creation of the world in the Bible chapters of Genesis, comparing it with the theory of evolution. I have heard sufficient sermons and watched numerous National Geographical documentaries to substantiate the authenticity of Noah's Flood. For instance, evidence found within the discoveries of marine fossils deposited on the peaks of the mountains within the regions of Andes and Alaska. I am sorry Mr Darwin, God wins!

In church, I learnt that the ageless Bible and the scriptures are formed by the breath of an Almighty, Supernatural God. In The Old Testament we have God in communication with Kings and Prophets. Then, Life was pure, sacred and sanctified through religious knowledge and traditional practices. Indeed, strengthened through a covenant by fulfilling the

Law to gain good standing with the Lord. At the same time traditional sin sacrifices that were performed to redeem their shortcomings, within the scope of their virtue, equally enabled them to regain their status of righteousness. Thus such purification and sanctification allowed a righteous God to descend to the earth and connect with the ordinary man. In the same manner, men received his blessings and goodness in covenant within such dedications. Here again, I would not doubt the historical figures such as Prophet Samuel, King David and King Solomon of Biblical times, who had recorded their encounters in the Book of Samuel, Books of Psalms and Songs of Solomon.

Sad to say, such practices of works done to fulfil the Law, eventually ended in more sins. For there were unobserved casualties, being descendants of Adam, as men were weak in flesh. For this reason, in sanctification, no one was able to achieve the hundred percent requirement to fulfil the Law. Neither by their righteousness in behaviour to upkeep the Law nor in the redemption through traditional methods, as they often failed after sometime. Within a matter of truth, God's righteousness could not be bought or earned by the works of men.

The New Testament is all about Christ Jesus, the Son of God who descended to earth as the Son of Man to rescue us and allow us to begin a new covenant with the Father. It was compiled partly by the Disciples of Christ Jesus, who had experienced life with him and who knew of his miracles, without doubt much done in the midst of their presence. Here Christ Jesus brought in the Gift of Grace to complement the Law, the pardoning or the forgiving factor. As a matter of fact, the obsession with the Law only brought dead fruits where Grace brought about good fruits. Grace is the beginning towards a journey of permanent transformation.

In Luke 7:37-48, within a parable of the two debtors, in comparison of one who owed a money lender 50 denarii, whilst another who owed 500 denarii. Jesus explained that whereas both were forgiven of their debts, in reality the woman who owed 500 denarii would love more. Similarly, in comparison within the same scripture, of the woman that Simon shun, as she sat at the feet of Jesus weeping continuously, while she anointed him with an expensive jar of alabaster oil. We know that she was much more grateful, even in her sinfulness, for she was forgiven much more. This certainly is a classic example that those whom are forgiven more would love more and would bring forth good fruits into the kingdom.

When Jesus died for us on the cross, he fulfilled the Law for all of us, clearing our sins forever. This allows us to gain our righteousness in standing towards God. The once unreachable God whom we could only access in our perfect statuette; now we could approach him without any fear of condemnation. Christ Jesus has taken all the wrath of the father on the cross, clearing and redeeming us of all our sins, since the days of Adam and including those of our future. As a result, we receive God's goodness and his inheritance, graciously justified by the unjust death of Christ Jesus, the sinless lamb at the cross, in exchange as our sin offering. Nevertheless, this does not give us a licence to sin, however it allows us to receive the gift of his mercy and grace to free ourselves. As much as there is evil in this world, there is also fragility. In Mathew 5:45 it reasons that the sun rises on the evil and good and the rain falls upon the just and the unjust. Everyone who seeks redemption in Christ Jesus, in times of need, will be saved. This comes from the place of his love for us and those who believe in Christ Jesus will never be forsaken, or his crucifixion would have been in vain. As much as we are worthy of his love so is he the worthiest "Our Son of God, Christ Jesus."

In Chapter Ephesians 1:18-21, therefore we see the glory of Christ Jesus in resurrection within God's love for us, *"I pray that the eyes of your heart may be enlightened in order that you may know the hope to which he has called you, the riches of his glorious inheritance in his holy people, and his incomparably great power for us who believe. That power is the same as the mighty strength he exerted when he raised Christ from the dead and seated him at his right hand in the heavenly realms, far above all rule and authority, power and dominion, and every name that is invoked, not only in the present age but also in the one to come."*

Therefore, we are bestowed in Grace, the unconditional reward, that comes with a fellowship with Christ Jesus. In addition, we receive the gift of the Holy Spirit. In John 14:26 it says *"But the Helper, The Holy Spirit, whom the Father will send in My name, He will teach you all things and bring to your remembrance all that I said to you."*

Sincerely, I believe this is new covenant of the Trinity, of the Father, Son & Holy Spirit, that would gradually lead us towards into a wholesome transformation together in our readiness to receive permanent goodness.

I am now convinced that I have a covenant with a Supernatural God. He has left me priceless knowledge of his promises and his inheritance through his prophetic words, that survived time tested days, allowing me the free privilege to discover them within the pages of a timeless book, **The Bible.** His thoughts are higher than us and his ways are higher than us. Therefore, when in trouble to bring forth the Ghost Busters to my rescue, I would cry out to Him, my God of Most High!

We *cry out* to *him*
        in different ways ...

We *know* *him*
        by different names ...

He *is* our ...
    El Shaddai
        The All Sufficient One, The
        Truth & Our Purpose ...

Adonai
> *Our Lord Master*

El Elyon
> *The God Most High*

Elohim
> *The Creator*

El Olam
> *The Everlasting God*

El Roi
> *The God who sees*

Immanuel
> *The God with us*

Elohim Shomri
> *My Protector*

Yahweh
> *Jehowah Lord of Truth*

Jehowah Nissi
> *The Lord my Banner*

Jehowah Tsidkhenu
> *The Lord is our Righteousness*

Jehowah Mekoddishkem
> *The Lord who sanctifies me*

Jehowah Raah
> *The Lord my Shepherd*

Jehowah Shalom
> *The Lord is my peace*

Jehowah Rapha
> *The Lord who heals*

Jehowah Jireh
> *The Lord will provide*

Jehowah Shammah
> *The Lord is there*

Jehowah Sabaoth
> *The Lord of Hosts*

Eloah
> **God Almighty**

In the Old Testament, God is known by different Hebraic names, not that there are many Gods. I am truly convinced that there is only One God, who created the Heavens & Earth. Men had a way of praising God in an alchemical way, in order to receive his goodness and his promises and it is within the human nature to pray as such. In the same manner as God is being praised by different meaningful names, consequently for this is precisely an affirmation that their prayers were being answered and giving thanks was due in the same traditional manner.

We find an example of this in Genesis 14:18, where the Hebraic name of God is mentioned, as "God Most High," namely in Hebrew, "El Elyon." In that particular scripture it mentions that, King Melchizedek of Salem brought out bread and wine to receive Abraham's gifts after the latter's victory, as the former was honoured, the "Priest of The God Most High."

The purpose that I included the Hebraic names, was to demonstrate that we have a time tested, Almighty God who is more than able, by means to supply to all our needs; heal our hurts; wipe away our tears; cure our afflictions; to protect and provide for us, as notably as a father would and much more, in addition to that, create miracles.

As in Jeremiah 29:11-13, God's promises of his plans for our future is something to meditate upon. Firstly, we need to invite him into our lives, as that enables him to will us his goodness and promises. Even though we have our covenant with a loving Father, we must realize that at the same time he has the persona of an ever righteous God, who hates the acts of sin. Sin comes with its consequences. Christ Jesus has intervened, in order to save us from its destruction. After his resurrection and in righteousness, Jesus now sits on the right of his Father's throne. He has the authority of power over all and the glory over the richness of the kingdom, that he has gained in accordance to his obedience. Thus, now as believers, we are able to receive the same righteousness through faith and receive the benefits of his richness and glory. For as Christ Jesus is, so are we in him and the Holy Spirit our comforter, consciously and subconsciously, reminds us of his words and works when we are in need. This is the imminent process towards our new identity in Christ. In such accordance, declare and receive your desired accomplishments in Jesus name. In the light of that, now we have a covenant with a righteous God who loves us unconditionally and is willing and able to give us the best. Praise Jesus!

Our Lord & Our Saviour...

John 10:22-29 *nkjv*
Now it was the Feast of Dedication in Jerusalem, and it was winter. And Jesus walked in the temple, in Solomon's porch. Then the Jews surrounded Him and said to Him, "How long do You keep us in doubt? If You are the Christ, tell us plainly." Jesus answered them, "I told you, and you do not believe. The works that I do in My Father's name, they bear witness of Me. But you do not believe, because you are not of My sheep, as I said to you. My sheep hear My voice, and I know them, and they follow Me. And I give them eternal life, and they shall never perish; neither shall anyone snatch them out of My hand. My Father, who has given them to Me, is greater than all; and no one is able to snatch them out of My Father's hand. I and My Father are one."

Philippians 4:6-7 *niv*
Do not be anxious about anything, but in every situation, by prayer and petition, with thanksgiving, present your requests to God. And the peace of God, which transcends all understanding, will guard your hearts and your minds in **Christ Jesus.**

Our Lord & Our Saviour

The Universe works on certain celestial codes. Codes that are based on the Laws of Cause & Effect that accordingly leads us on into diverse paths. In similar to that of the Law of Mathematics, ultimately we cannot change the fact that one plus one equals to two. The concoction of such laws were known to some ancient scholars and high priests, intelligent beings besides God himself, who have disappeared from the face of the earth. Therefore, the Biblical Laws are essential as a guide to our future as they are a reminder to the repercussions within the web of cause & effect. As such, man was given the freedom of choice by our creator. Our choices determine the next course of events based within the such law of orderliness of the universe. This is a secret that is only known to our creator.

Thus in history, Adam failed in the obedience towards God in the Garden of Eden. In the beginning, God intended Heaven for his children. Unfortunately, Adam sinned in collaboration with Eve, making a personal choice of eating the fruit from the tree of Knowledge of Good & Evil. Even though, initially Adam & Eve inherited all of God's creation within the Garden of Eden, without needing to labour for its goodness; they made a wrong choice without the needed wisdom. Regrettably, the needed wisdom of abiding towards the obedience in God. God had given them access to everything in the garden except to have the fruit from the forbidden tree and however, they chose to eat it. Soon afterwards, Adam & Eve fell from their grace, and so did the future of mankind.

Unfortunately for us, both of them were devised into treachery by the evil serpent, which was scheming towards dominion over God. This resulted in the course that man from then onwards would have to work by the sweat of his brow, in other words labour for his sustenance. Genesis 3.19. This was the beginning of the friction between man & God. Thereafter, man and his future generations had to bear the curse of sin, until Jesus appeared as our Saviour. God, in accordance to the law, had to banish both Adam & Eve from the Garden of Eden. Thus, consequences of such follies, the wisdom of man's choices and their results within the web of the cause and effect were recorded in the Old Testament. Furthermore, such scriptures enlighten us with an insight into God's righteousness, his power and his compassion in relation with his earth children. Such, the Bible gives us the genealogical time line of the God's creation of the world starting from the Book of Genesis, right until the end of times, revealed in the Book of Revelation.

Besides its artistic aspect, my next intention in the creation of this book was to bring about the essence of our Covenant within the Trinity; The Father, Son & Holy Spirit, in significance of our place and purpose in God's creation. To achieve such magnitude of orderliness we need the Bible. The Bible affirms God's prominence over us, as it transcends the truth within the scriptures. The word that is brought alive, through the works and spirit of Christ Jesus. John 14:6 *"Jesus answered, I am the way and the truth and the life. No one comes to the Father except through me."*

God made man in his image and his likeness. He gave us the dominion over all the earth including every creature. Genesis:1.26. Consequently, there are many facts & figures on the internet about the deterioration of the present ecological situation of Mother Earth. Man is not good at preserving God's creation, thus the world has come to a state of desolation. We need the supernatural powers of our Creator to work within man, therefore to reverse the destruction done by man. We need a revival of God's promises. We need him to work his will within every one of us. The ecological condition is only one of the many situational issues that we have to deal with today. We have many more immediate issues that are prevailing ranging from; poverty, diseases, afflictions, homelessness, human trafficking and thousands of refugees who are being driven out of their natural homes. This is not what God had intended for his beloved children, whom he created with much love. It saddens my heart to see such sufferings and pain. We can't hold the whole world in our hands and even if we tried, it would to slip away. But I know that I have a Lord, the Almighty One, who created the world from nothing and he is able to restore it. He has given us the gift of the Holy Spirit and through collective prayers, within his promises we could reverse almost any ruinous situation. In addition, understanding the essence of Jesus as the Son of God, unlocks a secret key to our sustenance and existence within the labyrinth of the Universal Law & Order.

Jesus Christ Our Saviour

John 14:6 *niv*
Jesus answered, "I am the way and the truth and the life. No one comes to the Father except through me.

Revelation 22:13 *niv*
I am the Alpha and the Omega, the First and the Last, the Beginning and the End.

Matthew 16:15-18 *niv*
But what about you?" he asked.
"Who do you say I am?"
Simon Peter answered,
"You are the Messiah, the Son of the living God."
Jesus replied, "Blessed are you, Simon son of Jonah, for this was not revealed to you by flesh and blood, but by my Father in heaven. And I tell you that you are Peter, and on this rock I will build my church, and the gates of Hades will not overcome it.

1 John 4:7-18 *niv*
Dear friends, let us love one another, for love comes from God. Everyone who loves has been born of God and knows God. Whoever does not love does not know God, because God is love. This is how God showed his love among us: He sent his one and only Son into the world that we

might live through him. This is love: not that we loved God, but that he loved us and sent his Son as an atoning sacrifice for our sins.

Dear friends, since God so loved us, we also ought to love one another. No one has ever seen God; but if we love one another, God lives in us and his love is made complete in us.

This is how we know that we live in him and he in us: He has given us of his Spirit. And we have seen and testify that the Father has sent his Son to be the Savior of the world. If anyone acknowledges that Jesus is the Son of God, God lives in them and they in God. And so we know and rely on the love God has for us.

God is love. Whoever lives in love lives in God, and God in them. This is how love is made complete among us so that we will have confidence on the day of judgment: In this world we are like Jesus. There is no fear in love. But perfect love drives out fear, because fear has to do with punishment. The one who fears is not made perfect in love.

Jesus Christ Our Saviour

The essence of Jesus, as I task to describe this would be most challenging, as much that he is the Son of God and in contradiction he lived on earth as the Son of Man. Let's examine his birth lineage first, his undeniable sovereignty, before I could magnitude his works that have brought about the birth of his followers & Christianity. A way of life that has been transformational for over 2000 years.

A short detour here, for I definitely know that this book was ordained by some supernatural circumstances that I have no other explanation than to validate it with my faith in Christ Jesus. As such a result, writing this book I believe is a calling and my purpose. The unfathomable chain of circumstances that led to my experiences, and of accounts of those experiences, that had merely salvaged me from an almost impossible tragic state. Nonetheless, only to miraculously change with touch of favour from God. Hallelujah! This is the love and grace of a Living God, working within his beloved child, that I truly believe is my miracle. My miracle of "Parting of the Red Sea." I am grateful to Christ Jesus as he gives me the strength to push on further, Philippines 4:13, *"I can do everything through him who gives me strength."* As such, I believe that my setbacks are being turned into a launch pad in preparation to publish this book.

I need to make a rather important point here, as I was not born a Christian, and until the year 2011, my perspective of Christianity was that it was a religion and Christians were governed by the Ten Commandments. I tried to read the Bible as I was searching for the meaning of life but failed to comprehend the value in its depth. Often, I felt displaced during the mass service at the traditional Church. I rather preferred to enter the premises of an empty, silent Church. Then have my personal conversations with God about my troubles and seemingly find my peace, even though they lasted for a moment until my next encounter with the dreadful world. Most of my conversations were about the unfairness in my world and my hurts. I went there to release my anger and my helplessness, being entangled within the web that was being spawned by the combined works of those who thought that they were involved in the development of my situational life. I was caught within the web of the vicious manipulations that encumbers almost every soul, within the circle of the human race.

Sometime during my age of early forties, I decided that I would consider myself a Christian. When someone by chance questioned me of my faith, I would explain to them that I am a Christian at heart, as subconsciously I believed that I had to work towards perfection, which is admirable of course. But the matter of truth is, psychologically, that would be a disastrous recipe in seeking perfection, self-obsession sets in. In addition, we would be looking towards others around us in comparison and for acceptance. Thus, while working towards such perfection, we allow manipulation, confusion and eventually exhaustion creeps in, as we would be trying too hard. Then afterwards, seek therapy of quick fixes like spending lots of money on spas, clothes, and stuff that we don't need. As a result, I was living in a zombie world. It seemed like a normal neighbourhood, likewise almost every one lived there. The tabloids, the magazines, the stores, friends & relatives. I was struggling to be perfect in a world that was not perfect.

Eventually I realized, that acceptance of non-perfection would be the ultimate cure and I was blind to that factor. Being peace loving and non-confrontational, even within my highest threshold, notwithstanding the struggle of juggling my life and pleasing everyone was killing me from the inside.

Ironically as it was, I believed in God, but did not know how to worship him and I did not have the right perspective of Christ Jesus in regards to whom or what he represented. I did not have a covenant with a communion, with a God Most High. Until recently, I presumed that the term, The Father, Son, and Holy Spirit, represented the sign of the Holy Cross, of which the congregation hand gestures within the premises of the church while in prayer, inclusive of upon entering and leaving the church. My idea of Christianity was still pretty close to the concept of Paganism, just that somehow, intuitively I was always mysteriously drawn back to the empty church. Periodically, such I returned to it and without much knowledge, I placed Christ Jesus among the other Martyrs of the world. In the light of the truth of a perspective, then I did not know him or his essence of his love for us as the Son of God. If you knew his essence you would want to journey with him too, forever & forever.

Now, returning to some historical facts and the birth lineage of Christ Jesus. The account of this, to the best of my knowledge is from the Book of Matthews. To start with, let us consider these two prominent figures in the Bible, namely Abraham & David. Christ Jesus was a descendant of both of these historical, biblical figures. His first ancestor Abraham, was from the lineage of Seth, third child of Adam & Eve. Even after Adam & Eve were banished from Eden, God still loved them and within his responsibility, had a relationship with their descendants. God's most monumental promises in the Bible was to Abraham and we could find that in Book of Genesis. Specifically, in Chapter 17, we find that Abraham & Sarah were given the gift of a child. The miraculous factor that Abraham was almost 100 years and Sarah 90 years of age. What caught my interest in that chapter was God invited Abraham to walk with him blameless as he revealed himself as "God Almighty," He then spoke to Abraham about obedience and his covenant. Here I strongly believe that God gave Abraham a way out from the ancestral curse that previously broke God's covenant with Adam & Eve, because of their disobedience to him. He offered them a new covenant through circumcision of all male infants of eight days. He wanted their obedience to him to be sanctified through circumcision. I'm sure God was more interested in the obedience of Abraham and his off springs, rather than the tradition of circumcision itself, as man did not have adequate wisdom to rule his affairs without the guidance of a God Almighty. I believe that an all-knowing God, who knew the heart wavering weakness and imprudence of men, in fairness wanted a show of the firm furtherance towards his loyalty from his earth children. Furthermore, it gave man something to identify in flesh, in regards to his obedience to an Almighty God. When Adam & Eve made that one wrong choice in the Garden of Eden, seemingly it must have scarred God deeply, as he must have lost his trust in mankind and doubted their obedience towards him. This time around, his covenant to man came with a small price in flesh through the tradition of circumcision. Besides, he promised his everlasting covenant with Abraham and his future generations with the gift of abundance; "land of their sojourning, all the land of Canaan." Now, we can receive the same Abraham's blessing with our new covenant with God, within the concept of a Trinity without the circumcision, through his son Christ Jesus.

When I was a rather young child, I must have read the story of David and Goliath numeral times, for the reason as it was included among many famous bed time fables. Prospectively, an illustration towards children, the possibility of minuscule strength and its potential might. Unrightfully, I had not heard or read it from the perspective of the Bible. Here rightfully, David the King who was previously a young shepherd boy, within the chapters of the Bible, gave us seventy-three beautiful works from the Book of Psalms. Reading both Book of 1 Samuel & Book of 2 Samuel, indeed gives us the almost a full account of David's life. David's story, without doubt, is considered a marvel of rag to riches. His life story is a true life drama, almost equivalent to those at the movies that one could hitch in search of entertainment.

Christ Jesus's second prominent ancestor David began his life looking after his family's sheep within the compounds of his father's field. There were many similarities in their nature. Firstly, David was from the city of Bethlehem. David was first anointed by Samuel the Prophet, and the declaration to anoint him came from the Lord All Mighty. When Samuel requested Jesse to bring forward his sons and as Jesse had eight sons, David being the eighth and the youngest was tending to their sheep away at the fields. Samuel, an anointed Prophet himself, did not anoint any of the seven sons that were first presented to him. Then the Prophet asked Jesse if he had any other son and thus David was summoned to him. Finally, when David arrived, Samuel discerned that it was he that was to be anointed. 1 Samuel Chapter 16, gives us the interesting account of this.

Next, with the anointment came God's favour and blessings. David was employed by King Saul to be the court's musician and he was recommended in excellence, as a man who was skilful in "playing the lyre, a man of valour, a man of war, prudent in speech and a man of good presence and the Lord was with him."

The most crucial factor that I wanted to highlight in the 1 Samuel Chapter 17, was why the Lord favoured David. No one was able to accept the challenge of Goliath, the much feared giant of the Philistines, but David offered to fight Goliath. He even went as far as to rebuke Goliath without any fear. Saul tried to caution David that Goliath was stronger, older and had much experience fighting in battles, while he reminded David that he was a young shepherd boy without any experience. David then reassured the King by giving him accounts of his experiences, such of those, while he tended to his father's sheep. As in

1 Samuel 17:34-36, *"But David said to Saul, your servant used to keep sheep for his father. And when there came a lion, or a bear, and took a lamb from the flock, I went after him and struck him and delivered it out of his mouth."*

What a revelation, seemingly in the previous chapter, while Samuel first wondered of whether to anoint the elder son Eliab, this is what he heard the Lord say professedly in

1 Samuel 16:7, *"But the Lord said to Samuel, "Do not look on his appearance or on the height of his stature, because I have rejected him. For the Lord sees not as the man sees: man looks at the outward appearance, but the Lord looks at the heart."*

Hallelujah! Praise the Lord! David was rightly chosen to be anointed under the guidance of the Lord, as he had the heart and the valour, similar to that of Christ Jesus, who has been courageously willed to rescue his lambs from Roaring Lions!

In comparison to David, Christ Jesus is the superior "Son of God," whose anointed courage was in the obedience of the word of his Father, that brought salvation to many. Here I would like to expand a truth of an enigma, without doubt it was his unbreakable covenant with the Father in Heaven that changed the course of the world, the cornerstone that resurrected men into Christians, including great Philosophers, Scientist and Leaders who have shaped and ruled the world through the word of God.

The Book of Luke, much solemnly describes his communion with the Lord and of the crucial incident that took place within the Mount of Olives. Where Jesus knelt down in an agonizing prayer as his sweat fell like drops of blood. There Jesus prayed to the will of the Father and dutifully surrendered his own will, much as he knew that the Temple

Guards would be arriving to arrest him and he would be betrayed by his Disciple Judas. I'm sure Jesus knew of the cruelty of the crucifixion that was at the hands of his enemies.

Christ Jesus must have realized the truth that men in flesh, are weak and susceptible to the sufferance of worldly pain and often found their escape in temptation. Likewise, he thought the same of his Disciples, even though they knew the way of salvation but lacked the ultimate faith that was required. The ultimate "faith that even as small as the mustard seed could move mountains" and such it would require patience and perseverance. I'm sure there, our all-knowing Heavenly Father, knew that the miracles of all miracles had to take place, to redeem the world forever. That was the only path that would bring forth the ordinary men to rise beyond their limitations and trust the Almighty God and wait for their deliverance. Furthermore, when coupled with such a faith in an Almighty God and in their righteousness in Christ, men would not have to resort to temptation and therefore salvation was at hand for everyone. I truly believe this is the reason why Christ Jesus gave in to the nature of the circumstances that was presented, as there was no other way and this was the only way. Here is the intensity of the scripture.

Luke 22:39-48 niv
Jesus Prays on the Mount of Olives
Jesus went out as usual to the Mount of Olives, and his disciples followed him. On reaching the place, he said to them, "Pray that you will not fall into temptation." He withdrew about a stone's throw beyond them, knelt down and prayed, "Father, if you are willing, take this cup from me; yet not my will, but yours be done." An angel from heaven appeared to him and strengthened him. And being in anguish, he prayed more earnestly, and his sweat was like drops of blood falling to the ground. When he rose from prayer and went back to the disciples, he found them asleep, exhausted from sorrow. "Why are you sleeping?" he asked them. "Get up and pray so that you will not fall into temptation."

Such with anointed courage Christ Jesus agreed to be crucified in obedience to his father, as he had the heart and valour to save his lambs, so that we could receive salvation and eternal life. Just like David, he delivered his lambs by means of Crucifixion and his Glorious Resurrection. Because of this, we are able to receive the gift of grace in mercy to resurrect within our failures, such as without condemnation we are able to continue within our status of our righteousness, as it still remains in the righteousness of Christ Jesus. Ultimately, we have been pardoned of our sins for once and forever without losing our Covenant with God. As he is an all knowing God who is compassionate to our misgivings, be at the same time he is a Righteous God who hates sin.

Therefore, this works in light of this truth of "Being Still" and with such tenacity in faith we could place our reliance upon him, in respect of his promises of all good things, while we rest upon him. To allow our Almighty God to fight our battles, simultaneously while we are in faith and find the strength to walk away from temptations and sins. Progressively, then to witness the miracle of the resurrection and receive the abundance of his richness and glory. Ultimately, receive them freely and watch such wonders work within our lives, without much effort.

As it is written in *Psalm 46:10*
> *He says, "Be still, and know that I am God;*
> *I will be exalted among the nations,*
> *I will be exalted in the earth."*

Now that we have establish Christ Jesus within his ancestral lineage, here is his magnificent life history.

Baby Jesus was born in the City of Bethlehem, in a manger. Both his parents, Mary & Joseph had to leave their hometown and as they arrived, there was no room vacant in the town of Bethlehem. According to the Book of Luke, Herod the Roman Emperor had asked for a census of the world. Therefore, Joseph had to return to the City of David as he belonged within the jurisdiction of the House of David.

Christ Jesus was born of a Virgin birth. As it is described in the Book of Mathew Chapter One, we find that Joseph was engaged to Mary, when it was established that she was to have a child, a miracle by the Holy Spirit. Next an angel of the Lord appeared to Joseph in a dream, assuring him that the infant, who is being conceived, is in fact from the Holy Spirit. The angel added that it would be a son, who was to be called Jesus and he would save his people from their sins. The angel reminded Joseph about an old prophesy by God to a Prophet; that a Virgin shall conceive and bear a son and they shall call him Immanuel, meaning "God with Us."

Three wise men who knew astrology and read the stars, came looking for Infant Jesus to worship him, as they too confirmed the prophesy of a birth of a "Ruler who will shepherd the people of Israel."

Here is a revelation! As a matter of fact, when an Omnipotent God, in specification, as he decrees to send his son to earth, would he not chose the most noble lineage and fashion his son after his favourite earth children? Something to think about …
God was on a mission!

Mary & Joseph once lost young Jesus, while attending an annual Passover Festival. They found him three days later and Jesus had spent those missing days at the temple courts, engaged in discussion with the teachers, who found him surprisingly bright. When questioned of his disappearance, young Jesus replied that he was at his "Father's House." Even though Mary & Joseph did not comprehend what Jesus meant, however Jesus must have known his identity in an instinctual manner at a very young age.

The missing 18 years the young Christ Jesus is still a very controversial subject. Being a mystery that baffles many scholars who are in research. I remember reading a book, "Jesus and The Essenes," by Dolores Cannon, a few years ago about a Jewish sect called The Essenes. I cannot confirm this with hard facts but the possibilities are there with this theory.

Earlier, the Roman King Herod with the intention to kill, was searching for the "Ruler who was to shepherd the people of Israel," when he was told of such a prophesy by the scribes. The normal reason for carnage among large empires, was the fear of the competition that would threaten their reign of succession. Such cruelty was practiced to retain succession within their own lineage. Since Jesus displayed such brilliance at the age of twelve in public places, subsequently he would have been a probable target. Even though Herod, The Great had died when Jesus was at a young age, I'm sure it was an equally dangerous situation to be found out by his descendants. I believe that he was sent away somewhere safe, away from the present ruling descendants of Herod.

During that period, there were three main Jewish sects namely, The Pharisees, Sadducees & Essenes. The Essenes were the purist of the group. They lived secluded from the other Jewish sects and believed in a life that enhances the value of Humanity. Therefore, the community of the such "brilliant scholars" existed away from the City of Jerusalem. I am very sure the Essenes have a very important link, that would explain the missing 18 years of the young Christ Jesus. Another interesting fact; The Dead Sea Scrolls were found in Qumran and this happened to be the City of the Essenes.

In Mathew Chapter Three, we first hear about Christ Jesus from John the Baptist, as he prepares the way to baptize him in the River Jordan. John introduces Christ Jesus as the one who is mightier than him, hence who would baptize them with the Holy Spirit, while John baptizes them with water. He also adds that as the water baptizes them for repentance, Christ Jesus with his winnowing fork will clear the threshing floor to gather the wheat into the barn, but the chaff he will burn with unquenchable fire.

25

Meaning, in fellowship with Jesus and through his word, coupled with the Holy Spirit, there will be a transformation within us that brings forth peace into our hearts through the obedience of faith. Even when we practice our freedom of choice, when faced by the temptation and evil, our thoughts and our actions will be that of wisdom. Through the word, our mind discerns in awareness of the scriptural goodness. The fellowship with Christ Jesus allows the Holy Spirit to work within us. As the Pilgrim progresses through his life journey, his soul transforms through a purgatory purification. Progressively, the transformed pilgrims will be gathered in the barn, that is to say we would have learnt to rest in the God Almighty, with a purpose in the life to bring forth good fruits within the Kingdom of God. To explain further, when we meditate in the goodness of the Bible, our actions will subconsciously be guided. We will find peace and we will be able to rest in the hope of his promises. This does not mean secluding ourselves in physical rest. This means that we armour ourselves with the word of God. Furthermore, the Holy Spirit will bring about miracles as we meditate and pray. God takes over our fights and rescue us, whilst Christ Jesus saves us from burning in the unquenchable fire.

Baptism is the beginning of a journey in fellowship with Christ Jesus in a covenant of faith, simultaneously to be enlightened in communion within the knowledge of the scriptures, in discovery of a Gracious, Supernatural and Living God. As we dwell within his promises, consequently the Holy Spirit works within us, bringing forth a wholesome transformation. We are on a journey of creating our own heaven on earth. The Baptism of Jesus is a significant occasion as there we first hear God acknowledging Christ Jesus as his Son. The heavens opened and the spirit of God descended on him, saying "This is my beloved Son, with whom that I'm pleased." Jesus was baptized at the age of 30.

Having said that, let us move on to some pivotal scriptures that gives us the insight of Christ Jesus within the perspective of him as "Son of God" who had descended to earth as "Son of Man."

Here I would like to reiterate that as we dwell upon these scriptures, some of these are my personal revelations received through our Father in Heaven. In addition to that, I am blessed with much privilege to be able receive such knowledge from amazing Grace Preaches on Sundays. Neither, am I a qualified Preacher nor a Theologian, however, I belief that our Father in Heaven loves us individually and he often sends us his love while in communication with us. Occasionally, when we need most his comfort, we receive such messages by the means of the scriptures through the Holy Spirit and in the name of Jesus.

The Temptation of Jesus
Mathew 4:1-11 esv

After his Baptism, the spirit let Jesus to the wilderness and there he fasted forty days & forty nights. During this time, he was tempted by the devil. I love this scripture as this amplifies The Trinity. Whenever in times of trouble, this particular scripture gives us an insight on how to relate the word in application. Here, Christ Jesus takes the persona of the ordinary man to show us the bridge that would connect us to the word. As such we could find our answer or comfort in troubled moments, within the scriptures, for they are the word of a Living God.

When the devil tried to challenge Christ Jesus, while riling about his identity that he was not the Son of God and that if so;

1. To turn the stones into loaves of bread.
2. To throw himself off the highest pinnacle of the temple of a holy city, so that God will command his angels to rescue him.
3. To worship the devil and thus receive the authority to reign the kingdom offered by the devil.

To all this he answered, "It Is written!" and he went on to quote these scriptures mentioned below. Another interesting revelation hidden in these scriptures, as Christ Jesus replied to the devil, uncovers the needed strength in purpose within our covenant with God and in such a manner that it drives away evil.

1. "It Is written! Man shall not live by bread alone, but by every word that comes from the mouth of God."
    Our Knowledge of God.

2. "It Is written! You shall not put Lord your God to test."
    Living in faith of God.

3. "It Is written! You shall worship the Lord your God and him only you shall serve."
    Love & Serve God.

Within these perspectives that with the valuable knowledge of the Bible, within its guidance we could live in faith, without fear and work towards God's will. The scriptures give us an opportunity to learn the time tested wisdom of the indispensable word. Accordingly, we would find supernatural strength, as in faith we grow further in life and in purpose. Our personal relationship with God is further being sanctified through the Holy Spirit and gives us a furtherance in obedience without any effort. Here Christ Jesus displays his confidence in the word, likewise we could equally make confident and not foolish decisions when tempted. Faith is the gift of God that enables us to move forward in life, even under unnatural circumstances, to bear good fruits and within our life journey with much good purpose.

Christ Jesus begins his Ministry

Christ Jesus began his ministry to save mankind from their dark circumstances and self-destruction. In Accordance to a prophecy in the Old Testament, he is the Light that Prophet Isaiah divined, whom would rescue the people of Galilee from darkness, as their lives were in midst of desolation and death.

Jesus calls the First Disciples
Mathew 4:18-22 esv

Christ Jesus first Disciples were Simon who was later known as Peter, Andrew, James & John. They all laboured as fishermen for a living. Christ Jesus could have conscripted anyone for his Ministry, anyone from the vast pool of learned men, instead he chose fishermen and made them "Fishes of Men." In my personal observation I noticed that Christ Jesus had a surpassing intellect, whom brought forth his poetic reason into life. An interesting impression that comes to my mind, is that Simon and Andrew would daily venture into the great ocean to fish from the depths of the unknown obscure waters. While, James and John laboured in arduous mending, often unable to forecast the damage of the nets, within an area of uncertainty, on the return of the fishermen after their catch from the sea. This sets out in rhyme a splendour of their nature revealed by Christ Jesus's ingenuity, specific knowledge coupled with an insight, that crumbling lives need the embrace of tenderness. Simultaneously, as they are gathered home, a need for such loving nature to surround them, before they could mend their own brokenness. Furthermore, both works were laborious, in need of great skills such as patience and faith.

There are two more phenomenal aspects of Christ Jesus magnificent works that I would like to deliberate. They would be about his well-known empowering Sermon on the Mount and the Healings and Miracles he accomplished during his lifetime on earth as "Son of Man." In the Book of Mathew, you will find the Sermon on the Mount within Chapters Five, Six & Seven paged before his Miracles & Healings. I shall embrace a few interesting scriptures. Thus, here are the Sermon on the Mount.

Sermon on the Mount

Beatitudes
Mathew 5:1-12 esv

There is beauty in compassion. Here Jesus says "Blessed are the poor in spirit, for theirs is the kingdom of heaven." "Blessed are those who mourn, for they shall be comforted." "Blessed are the meek, for they shall inherit the earth." "Blessed are those who hunger and thirst for righteousness, for they shall be satisfied." "Blessed are the merciful, for they shall receive mercy." "Blessed are the pure in heart, for they shall see God." "Blessed are the peacemakers, for they shall be called sons of God." "Blessed are those who are persecuted for righteousness sake, for theirs is the kingdom of heaven." "Blessed are you when others revile you and persecute you and utter all kinds of evil against you falsely on my account. Rejoice and be glad, for your reward is great in heaven, for so they persecuted the prophets who were before you."

Whenever I read the Beatitudes, there is an unexplainable calmness and peace that comes over my heart. This is a beautiful lullaby that Christ Jesus has bequeathed us, for comfort. Reflectively, sometime or somewhere, we might have been unjustifiably victimized within some menaced situation and would need comfort. Within our nature, we do not have the ability to gage the level of someone else pain except that of our own. Reactively with the onset of our own pain, an immediate response would be to seize the nearest person, and possibly validate away our problems and its issues in seek of relief. I encourage sharing, consequently its effectiveness very much depends on the wisdom of that particular friend or person or the lack of it. On the downside, our next level of manic might set in. Here, at the same time if we are able to redirect our energy into the wisdom of the scriptures, subsequently that would change our persona, possibly this could save us from taking any unwanted action that might be of a regrettable sin.

The great literary writer, C.S Lewis quoted that "God, who foresaw your tribulation, has specially armed you to go through it, not without pain, but without stain." The exquisiteness of this, is the reminder that within the depth of our pain and growth in wisdom, we have a Covenant with a great God. He is able to give us the world and as we to return to him, helpless as his child, in realization that we need his love, comfort and his promises. Therefore, it helps us to seek comfort within his scriptures and realize his love for us, as our Father in Heaven.

Salt & Light
Mathew 5:13-16 niv

Salt, within its purity has amazing properties. When God created salt, its purpose was to preserve the sea and its living organisms within it. Men then enhanced salt and created a domestic value and such now we are open to its many other purposes. Nevertheless, the salt did not lose its initial property for God's purpose. On our birth we arrive naked and bare, within God's intended identity for us. God created us with a purpose. His purpose was for us to work towards his glory and preserve his kingdom. Infants are considered a bundle of joy, hence they fulfil that joy, just being themselves. Thus our primary duty is to spread that joy to others. Everything else was added later, our clothes, our education, our homes and so forth. If under harsh circumstances, all these added on items were taken away from us, subsequently could we retain the original saltiness in us? If we are not planted in realization of our worthiness in the love of our creator, the matter of the truth is we will not be able to survive such harshness. In the long run, we lose our flavour in life. In reality, knowing that we have a Father God who loves us, places us in self-preservation. Thus, knowing God's love and his goodness over us, we will not let others trample over us. Thus as we live in Christ, no matter what our surroundings are, we will always be the **Salt of the Earth**.

Light that is elevated shines the furthest. When someone discovers our goodness, and has been touched by our genuine love and friendship, chances are that we would be given the best seat in the house. Thus, the followers of Christ Jesus, subsequently in covenant, receive the favour of the Lord, his communion and the anointment of his Holy Spirit. Meditating in the word, further adds a natural shine that glows within us. We are often attracted to others and thus opportunities, grace & favours are always imminent in our lives. The right doors open and we will be prominent within our family, community and will reign in life. We receive special royalty status for we are the children of the God Most High. Therefore, we will outshine darkness and will always be the **Light of the World**.

Do not be Anxious
Mathew 6:25-34 esv

Have you ever had an opportunity to sit on the top of a cliff and look over a scenic view of any particular landscape in its original natural state. One that is untouched by the architectural sophistication of men. In such quietness, I have often felt peace with the presence of God. Worrying is something that comes automatically to us without any need or practice.

Most of the time the underlying truth, compasses towards our fear that threatens our sustenance. Basically, triggered by the overwhelming onset of responsibilities towards our needs and that of our family. Fear creeps in when we face a situation that might threaten the source of our livelihood. Such fear could also be prevalent in other matters of acceptance. These may include matters such as in our appearances, the clothes we wear, our relationships, maintaining healthy lifestyle and our communal safety. Besides fear, competitiveness and the need of approval, are some of the common issues of non-acceptance that could be included in the list that may bring about sleepless nights.

Here Christ Jesus reminds us that we have Our Father in Heaven, the creator, who is able to provide all good things, in a timely manner to substantiate our needs. We should meditate on his word and thus wait patiently on his promises. Then he reminds us about the beautiful creation within the circle of conservation, manifested by our Father in Heaven. He brings our attention to the birds in the sky, for they are not obsessed about the need to store away food in barns. I could not marvel enough of their faith in our creator to be fed daily, furthermore this faith reassures their freedom to fly as far as their flight takes them. He then compares the lilies of the field in their picturesque beauty, as they shine and glow in nature, within the beauty of the landscape. Bringing tremendous joy to those who journey by them, often wanting to catch such beauty on portraits. Christ Jesus further exclaims that their exquisiteness surpasses the adornment of Solomon, who was the richest among the Biblical Kings. The Lilies faithfully know that they are favoured and have the grace of God to provide them with everything that is required for their nourishment. Thus, we should stop worrying about our troubles and look at Christ Jesus to supply all the glories of our inheritance and that of which God has already reserved for us through our fellowship with him. Once we stop the worry, we will be as free as the bird in flight, simultaneously be glowing in health and brilliant in our ways. Thus **do not be anxious about your life.**

Ask & it will be Given
Mathew 7:7-11 niv

We live in a world that is in need of nourishments and possessions for our sustenance. Rightfully, when God created the world he had allocated his inheritance towards our wellbeing. In Book of Genesis, we learn that he gave men dominion over all creatures that are found in the sea, sky and ground. Unfortunately, there is disparity and complexity within the economics of wealth distribution and then there is the behaviour to accumulate excessive proprietorship, within the reason of satisfying extremity in taste and status. Most of which are often the results of personal choices and such behaviours being some of the reasons of why there is much poverty in the world today.

Nevertheless, God has promised his children such to ask, seek and knock to receive his goodness in abundance, for any good father would love to adore us with the best. Nonetheless, he adds in a word of caution to the phrase, "Be careful, what you wish for," to remind us the advantages of his gifts in comparison to that of our parents. The wisdom of most parents, when it is within our knowledge, for we will not give harmful gifts to our children. Consequently, we have an all knowing and an all seeing Father God, who gives us his goodness, at the right time, opening the right doors and closing the wrong ones. Therefore, when at times without the foresight of an unknown situation, it is best to pray according to his will for gifts and receive in abundance, for he only gives his children the best. Patience coupled with faith are some good virtues to endure, while we wait for his goodness, for his gifts last us a lifetime. Gifts that last a life time need to be cultivated within us. Be patient as he is always working behind the scenes to bring forth great things for his children. Therefore, **Ask & it will be Given.**

Miracles & Healings

Jesus changes water into wine
John 2:1-11 niv

Christ Jesus's first miracle was that he turned water into wine. Once, he attended a wedding in Cana, Galilee with his mother Mary & his Disciples. Mary went over to Christ Jesus and requested his help, as the wedding party ran out of wine. He in reply, told her not to involve him as his time has not come. Without considering his reply, Mary who was familiar with the works of her son, in confidence told the servants to follow his instructions. Here I find a few revelations within the midst of this miracle. Firstly, even though Mary & Jesus's Disciples already knew of his capabilities, Christ Jesus himself was not ready to perform miracles in public. Mary, being his mother, had much faith in him and his works. Furthermore, she had her confidence in the obedience of Christ Jesus, that he would conform. Secondly, the miracle was that from a perspective of creation. We can change milk to butter or cheese and it takes time and it could be done only if the substance is of a certain solid matter. Here, Jesus changed water, that is at state of condensation of Hydrogen & Oxygen; in actual air gases. Only God was able to create something from nothing and as God created the world in six days. Jesus created wine from water drawn from six water jars that were used for ceremonial washing. The process of changing grapes into wine takes time in measurement of years as they need to be aged. Here Jesus compressed time. To everyone's bewilderment the guests remarked in surprise that the best wine was served last, where it was a custom then to serve it first.

Therefore, this reminds us that our complete faith in Christ Jesus is the key to miracles and that within God's favour even in our nothingness, when placed in his hands, could turn into abundance of goodness.

Jesus Cleansers a Leper
Luke 5:12-16 esv

While Christ Jesus was preaching at one of the cities, a man full of leprosy approached him and begged him to cure him. Christ Jesus touched him and said this to the him, *"I will; be clean."* Immediately the leprosy left him. Then Jesus told him to not to let anyone know that he was cured by him. He further instructed him to present an offering to the priest according to a tradition of Moses, so that there is proof of his healings. The one thing that is prominent here is that, as the leper approached Christ Jesus, he had absolute believe in him. He believed in miracles and therefore with his faith he stepped out to Christ Jesus. Next Christ Jesus knew the cause of his leprosy was a repercussion of sin. Here, in revelation is a covenant between Christ Jesus and the leper. The leper stepped out in faith and Christ Jesus agreed, without any conditions, to heal him. Consequently, Christ Jesus declared his blessing over the leper. He did not ask the leper, "Will you be clean from now onwards," instead he blessed him with authority saying, "Be clean" bestowing the holy spirit upon him. The covenant began the moment the leper fell down in his knees and begged to be healed. There was no need for any confession, all Jesus needed was our submission.

The act of submission is that of remorse, whereas sadly there are those who apply confessions as a trade in for their sins. That is not the intention of our Father in Heaven. He wants a Heart Transformation and at the same time he is willing in his grace and mercy to accept our fragility and weakness. Therefore, within our covenant and while in communion, we could seek him for the goodness of the world. Boldly request in faith and submission and receive in abundance for all good things, for there shall be no place for evil to creep into our lives.

Jesus cures a Man with a Withered Hand
Mark 3:1-6 esv

There was a prevailing traditional Jewish law that no work should be performed on a Sabbath day. One day as Christ Jesus was teaching at the Synagogue, a man approached him to heal his withered, right hand. Even though it was a Sabbath day, Christ Jesus knew that he would be under the scrutiny of the Scribes and the Pharisees, in spite of that he healed the man's hand. Shortly before that, he turned to the group of scheming antagonists, constantly waiting for his slightest blunder with the law, who were ready to condemn him of his actions. Christ Jesus gave them resilient reasons for his action, for he knew the works and the love of his father. He is the direct representation of Our Father in Heaven. The Synagogue excelled in the tradition of the Law, subsequently forgetting that we have a compassionate and all forgiving God. As a matter of fact, the moment we reach out to him, without the consideration of time or place, he is willing to heal.

The Hebrew word for pardon and forgive is "nasa" & "celah" which means to lift away. As the man stretched out his hand, Christ Jesus was technically taking away the man's affliction of transgressions and restoring him. Christ Jesus is able to heal anyone, anywhere, any day, especially in his Father's house. His miracles are beyond space and time. This assures us that we do not have to wait upon the right time, as God's grace is within our reach anytime and anywhere. We need to reach out to him in complete faith.

Here we see the wonders of Christ Jesus, who was able to accomplish Godly miracles while he reigned on earth, and thereafter continued with greater miracles after his death.

The name Christian, refers to the followers of Christ and was first mentioned in the Bible in Acts 11:26. After the ascension of Christ, two of his disciples, Saul who was later known as Paul, together with Barnabas, taught the people of Antioch about the works of Christ. Here within the historical facts, the first disciples of Christ Jesus in Antioch were known as Christians.

Upon his resurrection after his crucifixion, Christ Jesus appeared to many of his followers. The Book of Mathew Chapter 28, gives us accounts of Mary & Mary Magdalene, who met him at his empty tomb. Later Jesus met his eleven disciples and in the Book of Luke Chapter 24, we see our resurrected Jesus, dining with his disciples.

Here, Christ Jesus after his resurrection, explains within this remarkable scripture of why the crucifixion had to take place.

Luke 24:44-51 esv. *Then he said to them, "These are my words that I spoke to you while I was still with you, that everything written about me in the Law of Moses and the Prophets and the Psalms must be fulfilled." Then he opened their minds to understand the Scriptures, and said to them, "Thus it is written, that the Christ should suffer and on the third day rise from the dead, and that repentance and forgiveness of sins should be proclaimed in his name to all nations, beginning from Jerusalem. You are witnesses of these things. And behold, I am sending the promise of my Father upon you. But stay in the city until you are clothed with power from on high.*
Then he led them out as far as Bethany, and lifting up his hands he blessed them. While he blessed them, he parted from them and was carried up into heaven."

Within the Book of Mathew 28:16-20 esv, here we have the Great Commission, the instructions from Christ Jesus to his disciples.

"Then the eleven disciples went to Galilee, to the mountain where Jesus had told them to go. When they saw him, they worshiped him;

but some doubted. Then Jesus came to them and said, "All authority in heaven and on earth has been given to me. Therefore, go and make disciples of all nations, baptizing them in the name of the Father and of the Son and of the Holy Spirit, and teaching them to obey everything I have commanded you. And surely I am with you always, to the very end of the age."

Such as in the scripture of the "Great Commission," his Disciples embarked on a journey and baptized new followers, such initiating them within the covenant and within the communion. His followers were baptized by name of the Father, and of the Son and of the Holy Spirit. He further reminded them to observe all of his teachings as he had commanded them. Mostly, he promised his presence among them until the end of time. Then finally in Bethany as he blessed them he parted from them as he was carried into Heaven. How great is our God!

I am not going touch the actualities of his crucifixion as I recommend that you watch the movie by Mel Gibson "Passion of the Christ." Such to experience his sufferance in the hands of vile men. The gruesomeness that escapes their compassion as they crucified the one Saviour, the Son of God, who was able to bring forth heaven to earth and return us the goodness of Eden. Even with my best of journalistic skills, no words could describe what happened, for his torment lasted from 9am to 3pm and without mercy.

I am grateful today for the love of our Father in Heaven, who painstakingly showed us that men in their blindness could lack so much in wisdom in their ways. As they resorted to crucify his son that was sent to earth as a Saviour. Notwithstanding the irony, that they used the same Law that was given to them by the Father, God who created heaven and earth and everything in it. And within such a conceit, use the Law in a wrongful manner, as a basis to crucify his Son, Christ Jesus, whom was sinless and blameless.

Within such an injustice and a truth, the Law failed profusely in the wrong hands of such vile men. In a matter of truth, that God had to resurrect Christ Jesus in his Righteousness to bring forth Grace in salvation of humanity. Therefore, God in an equivalent attempt, allowed us to witness the resurrection and at the same time, he created our new covenant with his Son, Christ Jesus. With the gift of such a fellowship, and in our righteousness in him, that we could be saved forever. The fundamental truth is that we have a merciful God in not a very merciful world of men.

Next turning our attention to a significant Disciple of Jesus who's worth more than a mention is Saul, who was later known as Paul. We learn that the resurrection of Christ Jesus roused his Disciples into deeper involvement of his teachings and such were recorded in the New Testament. Regrettably, there was much despair and petrifying persecutions of his followers. Of such a history was Saul, who was a Galilean by birth and came from a family of Pharisees, who later became a high ranking Roman soldier. Saul went on a witch hunt searching for followers of Christ Jesus and caused terror in persecution. He went on rummaging the Synagogues as he tracked them down, with the intention to persecute them, supposedly if found with any evidence of the teachings of the Christ Jesus. One day, during such a pursuit, along the road of Damascus, a great blinding light shown from the heaven and knocked him down, literally blinding him. Then he heard a voice call his name, "Saul! Saul! Why are you persecuting me?" Saul then questioned the voice and received an answer, "I Am Jesus, Whom You Are Persecuting," and such the voice of Christ Jesus replied and further instructed him, "But rise and enter the city and you will be told what you are to do." The soldiers who were travelling with him froze and were speechless for they could not see any one around except hear the voice of Christ Jesus. Then they carried him into the city. Thus for three days Saul was blind and he neither ate nor drank. Christ Jesus than appeared to his disciple Ananias in a vision and requested him to lay his hands over Saul, who was at that time in Tarsus, so that he could regain his sight. Ananias, refused for he knew that Saul was persecuting the Saints in Jerusalem and was given instructions by the high priest to arrest his followers and disciples. Christ Jesus insisted that Ananias should carry out his request as Saul was chosen by the Lord to further his teaching to the Gentiles, Kings and the children of Israel. In obedience, on arrival Ananias revealed to Saul that Christ Jesus had sent him. Subsequently, he placed his hands on Saul and cured him of his blind sight. He then baptized Saul by the Holy Spirit. From then onwards Saul who was later known as Paul, became one of Jesus's most revered Disciple who changed the course of his teachings, that it reached furthest and eventually it transformed the masses. Seemingly, Paul wrote the majority of the books within the New Testament; Book of Romans, First & Second Corinthians, Book of Galatians, Book of Ephesians, Book of Philippians, Book of Colossians, First & Second Thessalonians, First & Second Timothy, Book of Titus, Book of Philemon & Book of Hebrews. We could read in detail the Conversion of Saul in the Book of Acts Chapter 9.

Without doubt, I am convinced that Christ Jesus is the Son of God who was incarnated into earth as Son of Man, by the way of a Virgin Birth. To begin with, he fulfilled his purposed exemplary legacy within the laws of prophesy and by the imprints of the stars that validated his birth. Next, he relentlessly continued an everlasting covenant with God, his Father. During the course of his life, he fulfilled God's mission as the "Son of Man" to convince the ordinary men, our potential in perfect faith when in covenant with God. In light of a truth, that an ordinary man could unveil his own miracles in healings and goodness with the grace and favour of an Omnipotent God. Finally, as he was raised from the fire of the Miracle of Resurrection, accordingly he strengthened our faith to a cosmic truth that our Covenant with God is beyond death and eternal.

In another matter of a truth, Christ Jesus came to give us a new lease in life within a possible shift to begin a new relationship with God. Christ Jesus, the "Son of God" became the "Son of Man," so that the "Son of

Man" could receive a status with God as his children and thus we will be known as the "Children of God." Christ Jesus came to reunite us with Our Father in Heaven, forever as his children.

An undeniable actuality is that teachings of Christ Jesus, have survived wars and persecutions for almost 2000 years and is the armour that we need to adorn to bring forth the fruits of Eden back into our lives. Jesus is the Messiah and a sad factor I have learnt is that the Jewish community is still waiting for the Messiah, who would lead the people of Israel to the Book of Torah.

In a short research I found out that the Sermon on the Mount, in reference to Mathew Chapters Five, Six & Seven were the instructions taken from the Book of Torah. Jesus added the Spirit of Grace to the Law. In fact, as the Law on its own failed and brought about destruction and death, for the reason that no one could live within perfection under unsympathetic, inhumane life conditions. Christ Jesus complemented the Law with his touch of humanity, with Grace and Mercy, thus adding the factor of his compassion. He must have rationalised the failings of men while they battled within their nature in weakness and as they struggled in a world of inequality. He would have seen the unfairness among men as they displayed behaviours of obsessive powers. He must have witnessed their need for control among them and such misuse the Law against each other to have control over one another. Without Grace, the Law failed due to the fact of men's obsession over it. Moreover, the Law furthered men away from God instead of what he wanted, a unification with his earth children.

Christ Jesus, within his personification on earth as a "Son of Man" has been and will be a magnitude of a legacy forever. I believe that there is no other unconditional love that would surpass what he did for his believers of followers and disciples. Today he watches over every single one of us with such an unconditional love. His divine love lasts until the end of time. The word "forever", I am sure was conjugated in the Bible from the perspective of "Until the End of Time."

I know in a million years, I would never be able to portray the perfect picture of our Sweet Christ Jesus, who loves us much and forgives us much. Having said that, I hope you were able to comprehend the loveliness of the Son of God, within his loveliness as our Saviour. I am another simpleton who is journeying my life with him. Hope you journey with him too.

Therefore, in communion within a covenant, the next few pages will establish ourselves as the "Children of an All Mighty God." The gift of salvation received freely through the Righteousness of Christ Jesus.

If you are ready, here I would like to include a Salvation Prayer. Please declare this aloud and in believe.

I declare that Christ Jesus is my Lord & Saviour. I believe that he died at the cross and was resurrected to clear all my sins, and such now he brings forth my salvation. I accept Christ Jesus into my life and receive his righteousness. In his righteousness, I now declare that I am a child of an Almighty God. I now freely receive the goodness and blessing of our Almighty Heavenly Father.

Amen!

Praise Jesus! Welcome to the Kingdom of God! Now you are the child of an Almighty God.

Daily Communion

Start your Day
Glorious

Matthew 6:9-13 nkjv
In this manner, therefore, pray:

Our Father in heaven,
Hallowed be Your name.
Your kingdom come,
Your will be done
On earth as it is in heaven.
Give us this day our daily bread.
And forgive us our debts,
As we forgive our debtors.
And do not lead us into temptation,
But deliver us from the evil one.
For Yours is the kingdom and the
power and the glory forever.
Amen!

Psalm *23 niv*
The LORD is my shepherd, I lack nothing.
He makes me lie down in green pastures,

he leads me beside quiet waters,
he refreshes my soul.
He guides me along the right paths
for his name's sake.
Even though I walk through the darkest valley
I will fear no evil, for you are with me;
your rod and your staff, they comfort me.
You prepare a table before me in the
presence of my enemies.
You anoint my head with oil;
my cup overflows.
Surely your goodness and love will follow me
all the days of my life,
and I will dwell in the house of the lord
forever & forever ...
Amen!

Our Father,
Our Father, Creator of Heaven & Earth,
The God of the Most High.
I praise you Lord, for you are
Able & Almighty.
As you renew your grace & mercies
towards your child.
Father, keep us safe through this day
and place us at the right place and right time
I pray to you for wisdom, courage,
compassion & a heart to love, Father.
I thank you Lord for this good day, as
I receive all your goodness freely,
Through the righteousness of Jesus Christ
Our Lord & Savior
Amen!

Bed Time
Affirmations

Matthew 6:26-34 *niv*

Look at the birds of the air; they do not sow or reap or store away in barns, and yet your heavenly Father feeds them. Are you not much more valuable than they? Can any one of you by worrying add a single hour to your life?

And why do you worry about clothes? See how the flowers of the field grow. They do not labor or spin. Yet I tell you that not even Solomon in all his splendor was dressed like one of these.

If that is how God clothes the grass of the field, which is here today and tomorrow is thrown into the fire, will he not much more clothe you — you of little faith? So do not worry, saying, 'What shall we eat?' or 'What shall we drink?' or 'What shall we wear?' For the pagans run after all these things, and your heavenly Father knows that you need them. But seek first his kingdom and his righteousness, and all these things will be given to you as well. Therefore, do not worry about tomorrow, for tomorrow will worry about itself. Each day has enough trouble of its own.

Psalm 121 *niv*
I lift up my eyes to the mountains
where does my help come from?
My help comes from the Lord,
the Maker of heaven and earth.
He will not let your foot slip
he who watches over you will not slumber;
indeed, he who watches over Israel
will neither slumber nor sleep.
The Lord watches over you
the Lord is your shade at your right hand;
the sun will not harm you by day,
nor the moon by night.
The Lord will keep you from all harm
he will watch over your life;
the Lord will watch over your coming and going
both now and forevermore.
Amen!

Psalm 91:1-2 *niv*
Whoever dwells in the shelter of the Most High
will rest in the shadow of the Almighty.
I will say of the LORD, *"He is my refuge and my fortress,*
my God, in whom I trust."
Amen!

Daily Communion

I believe in choosing the right scriptures daily to affirm and remind me the closeness of Christ Jesus, who is working miracles within me. This is fundamental as it enables me to leave my troubles at his feet and free myself. I have a five-minute devotional time when I wake up, that gives me all the goodness that I need to start my day. On a bad day listening to a playlist of worship songs strengthens my heart and adds a rhythm on my feet.

My first scripture from Mathew 6:9-13 was directionally given to his disciples, by Christ Jesus, in instruction as of how to pray. Next Psalm 23 is a famous scripture that anoints me daily as my trust is in my Lord. The prayer "Our Father," is my personal prayer to Our Heavenly Father from a perspective of his daughter to receive his mercies and goodness.

Retiring to bed, instead with alcohol or any other sleep prescription, try these towards a healthier lifestyle. Mathew 6:26-34 reminds me that whatever the events of the day, God has got all our problems in his hands as I am his beloved. Psalm 121 reminds me that I have a God who watches over me, for nothing goes on without his knowledge with a reassurance from Psalm 91:1-2 that I dwell under the shelter of a Most High God and I could rest in faith in him as he is Almighty. Sleep well beloved child of the Almighty God and have a peaceful night.
Place your trust in the Lord in Jesus Name!

I am
the child of an Almighty God ...

my Purposes

Jeremiah 1:5 *niv*
Before I formed you in the womb I knew you,
before you were born I set you apart;
I appointed you as a prophet to the nations."

Mark 12:30-31 *niv*
Love the Lord your God with all your heart and with all your soul and
with all your mind and with all your strength. The second is this: Love
your neighbor as yourself. There is no commandment greater than
these."

Matthew 28:16-20 *niv*

Then the eleven disciples went to Galilee, to the mountain where Jesus had told them to go. When they saw him, they worshiped him; but some doubted. Then Jesus came to them and said, "All authority in heaven and on earth has been given to me. Therefore, go and make disciples of all nations, baptizing them in the name of the Father and of the Son and of the Holy Spirit, and teaching them to obey everything I have commanded you. And surely I am with you always, to the very end of the age."

1 Peter 1:3-9 *nkjv*

Blessed be the God and Father of our Lord Jesus Christ, who according to His abundant mercy has begotten us again to a living hope through the resurrection of Jesus Christ from the dead to an inheritance incorruptible and undefiled and that does not fade away, reserved in heaven for you, who are kept by the power of God through faith for salvation ready to be revealed in the last time.

In this you greatly rejoice, though now for a little while, if need be, you have been grieved by various trials, that the genuineness of your faith, being much more precious than gold that perishes, though it is tested by fire, may be found to praise, honor, and glory at the revelation of Jesus Christ, whom having not seen you love. Though now you do not see Him, yet believing, you rejoice with joy inexpressible and full of glory, receiving the end of your faith—the salvation of your souls.

in his Righteousness

Romans 3:21-28 *esv*

But now the righteousness of God has been manifested apart from the law, although the Law and the Prophets bear witness to it; the righteousness of God through faith in Jesus Christ for all who believe. For there is no distinction: for all have sinned and fall short of the glory of God, and are justified by his grace as a gift, through the redemption that is in Christ Jesus, whom God put forward as a propitiation by his blood, to be received by faith. This was to show God's righteousness, because in his divine forbearance he had passed over former sins. It was to show his righteousness at the present time, so that he might be just and the justifier of the one who has faith in Jesus. Then what becomes of our boasting? It is excluded. By what kind of law? By a law of works? No, but by the law of faith. For we hold that one is justified by faith apart from works of the law.

Hebrews 9:11-14 *amp*

But when Christ appeared as a High Priest of the good things to come that is, true spiritual worship, he entered through the greater and more perfect tabernacle, not made with hands, that is to say, not a part of this material creation. He went once for all into the Holy Place, the Holy of Holies of heaven, into the presence of God, and not through the blood of goats and calves, but through his own blood, having obtained and secured eternal redemption that is, the salvation of all who personally believe in him as Savior. For if the ceremonial sprinkling over defiled persons with the blood of goats and bulls and the ashes of a burnt heifer is sufficient for the cleansing of the body, how much more will the blood of Christ, who through the eternal Holy Spirit willingly offered himself unblemished that is, without moral or spiritual imperfection as a sacrifice to God, cleanse your conscience from dead works and lifeless observances to serve the ever living God?

Romans 6:23 *niv*
For the wages of sin is death, but the gift of God is eternal life in Christ Jesus our Lord.

Hebrews 1:3- 4 *niv*
The Son is the radiance of God's glory and the exact representation of his being, sustaining all things by his powerful word. After he had provided purification for sins, he sat down at the right hand of the Majesty in heaven. So he became as much superior to the angels as the name he has inherited is superior to theirs

embraced in complete Faith

Romans 1:17 *niv*
For in the gospel the righteousness of God is revealed
a righteousness that is by faith from first to last, just as it is written:
"The righteous will live by faith."

Matthew 17:20 *niv*
So Jesus said to them, "Because of your unbelief; for assuredly, I
say to you, if you have faith as a mustard seed, you will say to this
mountain, 'Move from here to there,' and it will move; and nothing
will be impossible for you. However, this kind does not go out except by
prayer and fasting."

i am free to Believe

Acts 16:29-35 *niv*
The jailer called for lights, rushed in and fell trembling before Paul and Silas. He then brought them out and asked, "Sirs, what must I do to be saved?"
They replied, "Believe in the Lord Jesus, and you will be saved—you and your household." Then they spoke the word of the Lord to him and to all the others in his house. At that hour of the night the jailer took them and washed their wounds; then immediately he and all his household were baptized. The jailer brought them into his house and set a meal before them; he was filled with joy because he had come to believe in God—he and his whole household.
When it was daylight, the magistrates sent their officers to the jailer with the order: **"Release those men."**

2 Corinthians 5:6-9 nkjv
So we are always confident, knowing that while we are at home in the body we are absent from the Lord. For we walk by faith, not by sight. We are confident, yes, well pleased rather to be absent from the body and to be present with the Lord. The Judgment Seat of Christ, Therefore, we make it our aim, whether present or absent, to be well pleasing to Him.

with anointed Courage

Philippians 4:11-13 *niv*
I am not saying this because I am in need, for I have learned to be content whatever the circumstances. I know what it is to be in need, and I know what it is to have plenty. I have learned the secret of being content in any and every situation, whether well fed or hungry, whether living in plenty or in want. I can do all this through him who gives me strength.

Mark 1:7-8 *nkjv*
And he preached, saying, "There comes One after me who is mightier than I, whose sandal strap I am not worthy to stoop down and loose. I indeed baptized you with water, but He will baptize you with the Holy Spirit."

2 Timothy 1: 7 *njkv*
"For God hath not given us the spirit of fear; but of power, and of love, and of a sound mind."

resting in divine Peace

1 Peter 4:13 *njkv*
but rejoice to the extent that you partake of Christ's sufferings, that when His glory is revealed, you may also be glad with exceeding joy.

1 Peter 4:16 *njkv*
Yet if anyone suffers as a Christian, let him not be ashamed, but let him glorify God in this matter.

Psalm 7:1 *njkv*
O Lord my God, in You I put my trust;
Save me from all those who persecute me;
And deliver me.

Psalm 46:10-11 *nkjv*
Be still, and know that I am God;
I will be exalted among the nations,
I will be exalted in the earth!
The Lord of hosts is with us;
The God of Jacob is our refuge.

Matthew 11:26-30 niv

Yes, Father, for this is what you were pleased to do.

"All things have been committed to me by my Father. No one knows the Son except the Father, and no one knows the Father except the Son and those to whom the Son chooses to reveal him.

"Come to me, all you who are weary and burdened, and I will give you rest. Take my yoke upon you and learn from me, for I am gentle and humble in heart, and you will find rest for your souls. For my yoke is easy and my burden is light."

ordained as a vessel of Salvation

John 4:7-26 *msg*

A woman, a Samaritan, came to draw water. Jesus said, "Would you give me a drink of water?" (His disciples had gone to the village to buy food for lunch.)

The Samaritan woman, taken aback, asked, "How come you, a Jew, are asking me, a Samaritan woman, for a drink?" (Jews in those days wouldn't be caught dead talking to Samaritans.)

Jesus answered, "If you knew the generosity of God and who I am, you would be asking me for a drink, and I would give you fresh, living water."

The woman said, "Sir, you don't even have a bucket to draw with, and this well is deep. So how are you going to get this 'living water'? Are you a better man than our ancestor Jacob, who dug this well and drank from it, he and his sons and livestock, and passed it down to us?"

Jesus said, "Everyone who drinks this water will get thirsty again and again. Anyone who drinks the water I give will never thirst—not ever. The water I give will be an artesian spring within, gushing fountains of endless life."

The woman said, "Sir, give me this water so I won't ever get thirsty, won't ever have to come back to this well again!"

He said, "Go call your husband and then come back."

"I have no husband," she said.

"That's nicely put: 'I have no husband.' You've had five husbands, and the man you're living with now isn't even your husband. You spoke the truth there, sure enough."

"Oh, so you're a prophet! Well, tell me this: Our ancestors worshiped God at this mountain, but you Jews insist that Jerusalem is the only place for worship, right?"

"Believe me, woman, the time is coming when you Samaritans will worship the Father neither here at this mountain nor there in Jerusalem. You worship guessing in the dark; we Jews worship in the clear light of day. God's way of salvation is made available through the Jews. But the time is coming—it has, in fact, come—when what you're called will not matter and where you go to worship will not matter.

"It's who you are and the way you live that count before God. Your worship must engage your spirit in the pursuit of truth. That's the kind of people the Father is out looking for: those who are simply and honestly themselves before him in their worship. God is sheer being itself—Spirit. Those who worship him must do it out of their very being, their spirits, their true selves, in adoration."

The woman said, *"I don't know about that. I do know that the Messiah is coming. When he arrives, we'll get the whole story."*

"I am he," said Jesus. *"You don't have to wait any longer or look any further."*

Just then his disciples came back. They were shocked. They couldn't believe he was talking with that kind of a woman. No one said what they were all thinking, but their faces showed it.

The woman took the hint and left. In her confusion she left her water pot. Back in the village she told the people, *"Come see a man who knew all about the things I did, who knows me inside and out. Do you think this could be the Messiah?"* And they went out to see for themselves.

creating Heaven on Earth

2 Peter 1 :2-3 *niv*
Grace and peace be yours in abundance through the knowledge of God and of Jesus our Lord. His divine power has given us everything we need for a godly life through our knowledge of him who called us by his own glory and goodness.

Romans 8:37-39 *niv*
No, in all these things we are more than conquerors through him who loved us.
For I am convinced that neither death nor life, neither angels nor demons, neither the present nor the future, nor any powers, neither height nor depth, nor anything else in all creation, will be able to separate us from the love of God that is in Christ Jesus our Lord.

Mark 11:24 *niv*
Therefore, I tell you, whatever you ask for in prayer, believe that you have received it, and it will be yours.

Matthew 5:13-16 *niv*
Salt and Light
"You are the salt of the earth. But if the salt loses its saltiness, how can it be made salty again? It is no longer good for anything, except to be thrown out and trampled underfoot.

"You are the light of the world. A town built on a hill cannot be hidden. Neither do people light a lamp and put it under a bowl. Instead they put it on its stand, and it gives light to everyone in the house. In the same way, let your light shine before others, that they may see your good deeds and glorify your Father in heaven.

1 Corinthians 13:4-7 *niv*
Love is patient, love is kind. It does not envy, it does not boast, it is not proud. It does not dishonor others, it is not self-seeking, it is not easily angered, it keeps no record of wrongs. Love does not delight in evil but rejoices with the truth. It always protects, always trusts, always hopes, always perseveres.

John **14:27** *niv*
Peace I leave with you; my peace I give you. I do not give to you as the world gives.
Do not let your hearts be troubled and do not be afraid

Isaiah 55 *esv*
The Compassion of the LORD
"Come, everyone who thirsts,
 come to the waters;
and he who has no money,
 come, buy and eat!
Come, buy wine and milk
 without money and without price.

Why do you spend your money for that which is not bread, and your labor for that which does not satisfy?

Listen diligently to me, and eat what is good,
 and delight yourselves in rich food.
Incline your ear, and come to me;
 hear, that your soul may live;
and I will make with you an everlasting covenant,
 my steadfast, sure love for David.

Behold, I made him a witness to the peoples,
 a leader and commander for the peoples.
Behold, you shall call a nation that you do not know,
 and a nation that did not know you shall run to you,
because of the LORD your God, and of the Holy One of Israel, for he has glorified you.

"Seek the LORD while he may be found;
 call upon him while he is near;
let the wicked forsake his way,
 and the unrighteous man his thoughts;
let him return to the LORD, that he may have compassion on him, and to our God, for he will abundantly pardon.

For my thoughts are not your thoughts,
    neither are your ways my ways, declares the LORD.
For as the heavens are higher than the earth,
    so are my ways higher than your ways
    and my thoughts than your thoughts.

"For as the rain and the snow come down from heaven
    and do not return there but water the earth,
making it bring forth and sprout,
    giving seed to the sower and bread to the eater,
so shall my word be that goes out from my mouth;
    it shall not return to me empty,
but it shall accomplish that which I purpose,
    and shall succeed in the thing for which I sent it.

"For you shall go out in joy
    and be led forth in peace;
the mountains and the hills before you
    shall break forth into singing,
    and all the trees of the field shall clap their hands.
Instead of the thorn shall come up the cypress;
    instead of the brier shall come up the myrtle;
and it shall make a name for the LORD,
    an everlasting sign that shall not be cut off."

I am a child of an Almighty God

I am a child of God for I have found my purpose formed in his righteousness thus I shall embrace in faith for i am free to believe that I am able to live my life with anointed courage and such resting in divine peace while ordained as a vessel of salvation thus creating heaven on earth ...

This is my personal experience; embarking on this life journey, without knowing our identity in Christ could be very challenging. It begins with recognizing that we are the children of an Almighty God, who now is officially our Father in Heaven with Christ Jesus and the Holy Spirit at his helm. He has sent every one of us to earth with a purpose.

Within a hypothetical concept, when fixing a large jigsaw puzzle, we often find all the pieces jumbled together in chaos before searching for the right piece. Once found, we would need to fit them at the correct pre-allocated space or in position to complete the big picture. Some of us go through the majority of our lives without knowing our purpose in him.

Let us say, there are many puzzles to be completed. Within such possibilities and our choices often shift changes our purpose. Thus this allows us to forget our original purpose and thus losing God's pieces to the devil. In such cases, Christ Jesus patiently waits for us to remember our true identity before he could complete the divine puzzle. Once we acknowledge Christ Jesus, and so forth we are automatically gathered into our Father's Kingdom. Within such a realm, Christ Jesus carefully shapes us back into our original purpose, as we need to trust him to do the work of our wholesome transformation, with the help of the Holy Spirit. Here, the Holy Spirit, our comforter brings us to the remembrance our covenant with our Father in Heaven and his promises.

On the other hand, if the devil completes more puzzles than our Lord, the world loses its equilibrium and that's when we see poverty, homelessness, earthquakes, floods and all kind of calamities. While Christ Jesus holds the world to heavenly places and the devil holds the places of hell.

Some of us prefer to sit on our laurels without taking any actions, as of our identity sways according to the directions of the wind, and are possibly within the risk factors of our own circumstances. The risk factor of a foundation that is built upon superficial and material value. Furthermore, it allows the possibility of our circumstance to dictate our values and our choices without much direction. Whereas, when we are gathered into the Kingdom of God, our identity is in Christ, meaning our foundation is built in him, within his values.

Another factor is that, when our life is centred around our own self-fulfilment, being a cause within a root factor of fear, that if we are not self-sufficient and fixatedly cautious, we would be considered a failure or would end homeless. I believe it is a legitimate fear factor, as the way some countries are governed without leaders who are compassionate to the cry of it citizens. The ways and teachings of Christ Jesus is a great leadership tool that could help various societies into reformation.

This might sound a kind of drastic, but I was hoping that this would give you an understanding of the repercussions of our complacency and none action, as the world belongs to every one of us and we should equally enjoy the inheritance of what our Heavenly Father has allocated to us.

Once we enter into the covenant with acceptance of Christ Jesus, simultaneously we establish ourselves as Children of the Almighty God. Then in communion of prayers, we could identify our God purpose with the help of the Holy Spirit. Our righteousness in Christ Jesus supplies us all the necessary factors of God's favours, grace, mercies and richness to be at the heavenly places on earth. The Heavenly places that has been proposed in that puzzle of life. To achieve that we must have the faith that we are loved and that we could receive God's promises, because he is a Righteous God and he would honour his son, Christ Jesus's suffering in crucifixion. Consequently, we need to declare that Christ Jesus has saved us and in his Righteousness, we deserve the goodness and promises of a Righteous God. This unrelenting faith will further bring us to a place of believe as we see miracles take place to fulfil God's promises. When we at such a place of believe, armoured with God's word and with wisdom, seemingly we walk around with anointed courage bringing good fruits into God's purpose without any fear of any retribution or condemnation. This allows us to rest in divine peace as we rest on the God Most High to fight our battles. Once our fear and anxiousness of a situation is taken away from us, we find our peace. In such a free state of mind, our God's purpose further emerges from within us. This further allows us to spread the same miracle that we have experienced to the rest of the world. Thus we become a vessel of salvation to others. We shine in God's light, bringing forth great treasures of the Kingdom and goodness will overflow in abundance into our lives. If you remember the promise of Christ Jesus in Luke 24:49 to his disciples, for he will not send us on missions until he clothes us with power from high. Therefore, meditate on his words and let the Holy Spirit work on us. In Mathew 11:30 he reminds us that "For my yoke is easy and my burden is light." It is a beginning of a miracle, our Wholesome, Heart Transformation. It is not by our works!

This is the miracle of Christ Jesus. This is the miracle of Life. This is the covenant of a relationship in communion with a Living God. This allows us to receive the key to every inheritance of Our Father in Heaven through the finished works of Christ Jesus at the cross. When we are joyful, in light within our purpose we are able to spread the same joy to others. We are given full rights to God's heavenly places, where it is safe and at the same time it holds his richness and his glory. We are **creating heaven on earth,** our personal heaven on earth.

the world

   is peripheral to

the Church ...

Job 38 *niv*

The LORD Speaks

Then the LORD spoke to Job out of the storm. He said:
"Who is this that obscures my plans
   with words without knowledge?
Brace yourself like a man;
   I will question you,
   and you shall answer me.
"Where were you when I laid the earth's foundation?
   Tell me, if you understand.
Who marked off its dimensions? Surely you know!
   Who stretched a measuring line across it?

On what were its footings set,
   or who laid its cornerstone,
while the morning stars sang together
   and all the angels shouted for joy?

"Who shut up the sea behind doors
when it burst forth from the womb,
when I made the clouds its garment
and wrapped it in thick darkness,
when I fixed limits for it
and set its doors and bars in place,
when I said, 'This far you may come and no farther;
here is where your proud waves halt'?

"Have you ever given orders to the morning,
or shown the dawn its place,
that it might take the earth by the edges
and shake the wicked out of it?
The earth takes shape like clay under a seal;
its features stand out like those of a garment.
The wicked are denied their light,
and their upraised arm is broken.
"Have you journeyed to the springs of the sea
or walked in the recesses of the deep?
Have the gates of death been shown to you?
Have you seen the gates of the deepest darkness?

Have you comprehended the vast expanses of the earth?

Tell me, if you know all this.
"What is the way to the abode of light?
And where does darkness reside?
Can you take them to their places?
Do you know the paths to their dwellings?
Surely you know, for you were already born!
You have lived so many years!
"Have you entered the storehouses of the snow
or seen the storehouses of the hail,

which I reserve for times of trouble,
    for days of war and battle?

What is the way to the place where the lightning is dispersed,
or the place where the east winds are scattered over the earth?

Who cuts a channel for the torrents of rain,
    and a path for the thunderstorm,
to water a land where no one lives,
    an uninhabited desert,
to satisfy a desolate wasteland
    and make it sprout with grass?
Does the rain have a father?
    Who fathers the drops of dew?
From whose womb comes the ice?
    Who gives birth to the frost from the heavens
when the waters become hard as stone,
    when the surface of the deep is frozen?

"Can you bind the chains of the Pleiades?
    Can you loosen Orion's belt?
Can you bring forth the constellations in their seasons
    or lead out the Bear with its cubs?
Do you know the laws of the heavens?
    Can you set up God's dominion over the earth?
"Can you raise your voice to the clouds
    and cover yourself with a flood of water?
Do you send the lightning bolts on their way?
    Do they report to you, 'Here we are'?

Who gives the ibis wisdom
    or gives the rooster understanding?

Who has the wisdom to count the clouds?
  Who can tip over the water jars of the heavens
when the dust becomes hard
  and the clods of earth stick together?

"Do you hunt the prey for the lioness
  and satisfy the hunger of the lions
when they crouch in their dens
  or lie in wait in a thicket?
Who provides food for the raven
  when its young cry out to God
  and wander about for lack of food?

Job 39 *niv*

"Do you know when the mountain goats give birth?
   Do you watch when the doe bears her fawn?
Do you count the months till they bear?
   Do you know the time they give birth?

They crouch down and bring forth their young;
   their labor pains are ended.
Their young thrive and grow strong in the wilds;
   they leave and do not return.
"Who let the wild donkey go free?
   Who untied its ropes?
I gave it the wasteland as its home,
   the salt flats as its habitat.

It laughs at the commotion in the town;
   it does not hear a driver's shout.
It ranges the hills for its pasture
   and searches for any green thing.

"Will the wild ox consent to serve you?
   Will it stay by your manger at night?
Can you hold it to the furrow with a harness?
   Will it till the valleys behind you?

Will you rely on it for its great strength?
Will you leave your heavy work to it?
Can you trust it to haul in your grain
and bring it to your threshing floor?

"The wings of the ostrich flap joyfully,
though they cannot compare
with the wings and feathers of the stork.
She lays her eggs on the ground
and lets them warm in the sand,
unmindful that a foot may crush them,
that some wild animal may trample them.
She treats her young harshly, as if they were not hers;
she cares not that her labor was in vain,
for God did not endow her with wisdom
or give her a share of good sense.
Yet when she spreads her feathers to run,
she laughs at horse and rider.

"Do you give the horse its strength
or clothe its neck with a flowing mane?
Do you make it leap like a locust,
striking terror with its proud snorting?
It paws fiercely, rejoicing in its strength,
and charges into the fray.
It laughs at fear, afraid of nothing;
it does not shy away from the sword.
The quiver rattles against its side,
along with the flashing spear and lance.
In frenzied excitement it eats up the ground;
it cannot stand still when the trumpet sounds.
At the blast of the trumpet it snorts, 'Aha!'

It catches the scent of battle from afar,
    the shout of commanders and the battle cry.

"Does the hawk take flight by your wisdom
    and spread its wings toward the south?
Does the eagle soar at your command
    and build its nest on high?
It dwells on a cliff and stays there at night;
    a rocky crag is its stronghold.
From there it looks for food;
    its eyes detect it from afar.
Its young ones feast on blood,
    and where the slain are, there it is."

Job 40 niv

The L*ord* *said to Job:*

"Will the one who contends with the Almighty correct him?
Let him who accuses God answer him!"

Then Job answered the L*ord:*

"I am unworthy, how can I reply to you?
I put my hand over my mouth.
I spoke once, but I have no answer
twice, but I will say no more."

Then the L*ord* *spoke to Job out of the storm:*

"Brace yourself like a man;
I will question you, and you shall answer me.

"Would you discredit my justice?
Would you condemn me to justify yourself?
Do you have an arm like God's,
and can your voice thunder like his?

Then adorn yourself with glory and splendor,
        and clothe yourself in honor and majesty.
Unleash the fury of your wrath,
        look at all who are proud and bring them low,
look at all who are proud and humble them,
        crush the wicked where they stand.
Bury them all in the dust together;
        shroud their faces in the grave.
Then I myself will admit to you
        that your own right hand can save you.

"Look at Behemoth,
        which I made along with you
        and which feeds on grass like an ox.
What strength it has in its loins,
        what power in the muscles of its belly!
Its tail sways like a cedar;
        the sinews of its thighs are close-knit.
Its bones are tubes of bronze,
        its limbs like rods of iron.
It ranks first among the works of God,
        yet its Maker can approach it with his sword.

The hills bring it their produce,
        and all the wild animals play nearby.
Under the lotus plants it lies,
        hidden among the reeds in the marsh.
The lotuses conceal it in their shadow;
        the poplars by the stream surround it.
A raging river does not alarm it;
        it is secure, though the Jordan should surge against its mouth.
Can anyone capture it by the eyes,
        or trap it and pierce its nose?

Job 41 niv

"Can you pull in Leviathan with a fishhook
or tie down its tongue with a rope?
Can you put a cord through its nose
or pierce its jaw with a hook?
Will it keep begging you for mercy?
Will it speak to you with gentle words?
Will it make an agreement with you
for you to take it as your slave for life?
Can you make a pet of it like a bird
or put it on a leash for the young women
in your house?

Will traders barter for it?
Will they divide it up among the merchants?

Can you fill its hide with harpoons
or its head with fishing spears?
If you lay a hand on it,
you will remember the struggle and never do it again!

Any hope of subduing it is false;
the mere sight of it is overpowering.

No one is fierce enough to rouse it.
  Who then is able to stand against me?
Who has a claim against me that I must pay?
  Everything under heaven belongs to me.

Who can strip off its outer coat?
  Who can penetrate its double coat of armor?
Who dares open the doors of its mouth,
  ringed about with fearsome teeth?
Its back has rows of shields
  tightly sealed together;
each is so close to the next
  that no air can pass between.

They are joined fast to one another;
  they cling together and cannot be parted.
Its snorting throws out flashes of light;
  its eyes are like the rays of dawn.
Flames stream from its mouth;
  sparks of fire shoot out.

Smoke pours from its nostrils
  as from a boiling pot over burning reeds.
Its breath sets coals ablaze,
  and flames dart from its mouth.
Strength resides in its neck;
  dismay goes before it.
The folds of its flesh are tightly joined;
  they are firm and immovable.
Its chest is hard as rock,
  hard as a lower millstone.

When it rises up, the mighty are terrified;
they retreat before its thrashing.
The sword that reaches it has no effect,
nor does the spear or the dart or the javelin.
Iron it treats like straw
and bronze like rotten wood.
Arrows do not make it flee;
slingstones are like chaff to it.
A club seems to it but a piece of straw;
it laughs at the rattling of the lance.
Its undersides are jagged potsherds,
leaving a trail in the mud like a threshing sledge.
It makes the depths churn like a boiling caldron
and stirs up the sea like a pot of ointment.
It leaves a glistening wake behind it;
one would think the deep had white hair.
Nothing on earth is its equal
a creature without fear.
It looks down on all that are haughty;
it is king over all that are proud."

our saving Grace

John 15:7 *nkjv*
If you abide in Me, and My words abide in you, you will ask what you desire, and it shall be done for you.

Romans 10:8-10 *niv*
But what does it say? "The word is near you; it is in your mouth and in your heart," that is, the message concerning faith that we proclaim: If you declare with your mouth, "Jesus is Lord," and believe in your heart that God raised him from the dead, you will be saved. For it is with your heart that you believe and are justified, and it is with your mouth that you profess your faith and are saved.

Therefore, Praise Jesus

The world is Peripheral
to the Church

The reason why I included the scriptures from Job 38 to 41 was because of its poetical and theatrical essence and to add a touch of humour of how impressive the works of God are compared to the ordinary man. Supposedly, as without Christ Jesus we would not be able to stand the magnificence of God in his Righteousness.

The scriptures in the Book of Job, were named as the greatest poem of ancient and modern times by Lord Alfred Tennyson, a great poet.

Here, we see a Mighty God, who tested Job of his loyalty. His love for Job was definitely evident to me, as we have a God who is Supreme as he knows the individual strength of all his children. God was battling with Satan about Job's loyalty. Satan chided God that Job loves and favours God only because of his richness and blessings he receives. Therefore, to test Job, God took away all his blessing. Nevertheless, Job kept his faith till the end. Eventually God won and Satan lost, as Job did not waiver in his faith and was restored all that was taken away from him. Thus we have the greatest poetry ever written in the Bible.

Without God there is no world. God created the church through his son, Christ Jesus to hold the world. The world belongs to God and we his children receive his inheritance on earth as we inhabit in it. Then comes the time that we progress on to the ether place called Heaven. In the course of history, we have seen High Priest or Noble men, with cosmic knowledge, whom have guided royalty since ancient times.

Therefore, the **world is peripheral** to the church, precisely that the church belongs to our God Almighty.

Our Saving Grace

Taking into consideration that Christ Jesus is offering us a new lease of life through his death and resurrection within a new covenant. Romans 10:8-10 allows us his salvation and fellowship through a Salvation prayer. Saying this prayer aloud and in believe within your heart, thus you will be saved.

I declare that Christ Jesus is my Lord & Saviour. I believe that he died at the cross and was resurrected to clear all my sins, and such now he brings forth my salvation. I accept Christ Jesus into my life and receive his righteousness. In his righteousness, I now declare that I am a child of an Almighty God. I now freely receive the goodness and blessing of our Almighty Heavenly Father.

Amen!

Praise Jesus! Welcome to the Kingdom of God! Now you are the child of an Almighty God.

Praise Jesus!

The Revival of Humanity

I am a believer of Christ Jesus and for now sure know that in application of his Life and Teachings, I could use my God given potential to the fullest. I have also learnt that this does not mean perfection. None who are in flesh would be able to live perfectly in Christ either.

Christ Jesus died and was resurrected to give us lifetime of free passes, and neither would I use them in intention to sin. Jesus allowed himself to be crucified for the very reason that mankind should be freed from sin, the cause of the ripple effect and pain that causes enmity and much pain between us and others. It also entangles us in a web of none ending deceit and keeps us in the past. The revival in Christ allows us to move forward into the future. We are able to forget our past and start again with a clean slate. This is the best psychological remedy and Jesus has ordained that for us within his ingenuity. Nonetheless, declaring our righteousness in God through Jesus, allows us the state of Christ, within us. This mindset allows us to progress within God's kingdom, while we receive his promises of all good things. Furthermore, God hates sin, and at the same time he loves us much.

It is great when we are able to swim in the lap of luxury and do not know anything about the life that goes through dirt and grime, where much of poverty lives. Blessed that some of us are able to receive our generation blessings and pray that such a life gives us the moments of clarity and goodness.

Nevertheless, now more than ever we need to start somewhere in preservation. A new generation of grace based churches are on the rise and a new generation of youth are on the rise. As much as a college degree is pursued after, I pray that the present youth find the right kind of church that dwells and armours them with the grace based teachings and receive their inheritance, goodness and transformation within the realms of the Father, Son & the Holy Spirit in anointment. In addition, for starters, I recommend listening to sermons of these amazing grace preaching Pastors, such as Joseph Prince of New Creation Church, Brian & Bobbie Houston of Hillsong Church, Joel & Victoria Osteen of Lakewood Church. I continuously listen to God's word and it has brought much good fruits into my life and has been transformational.

There is much more between the pages of the Bible, such without doubt that could give you the thrills of a novel or a movie. I often feel sad when Christianity is often portrayed by both Christians and Non-Christians as a religion, thus provoking communal disharmony. Christianity is a way of life and it is a way of peace. It is a life giving and we have a Living God who loves us till the End of Time...

In Colossians 3:15-17 niv
"Let the peace of Christ rule in your hearts, since as members of one body you were called to peace. And be thankful. Let the message of Christ dwell among you richly as you teach and admonish one another with all wisdom through psalms, hymns, and songs from the Spirit, singing to God with gratitude in your hearts. And whatever you do, whether in word or deed, do it all in the name of the Lord Jesus, giving thanks to God the Father through him."

Dear Beloved,
Child of an Almighty God.

Hope you enjoyed your journey throughout this precious creation.

As I am a child of an Almighty God of the Most High, with much faith, I believe that this book will reveal your true identity in him and will be the beginning of many miracles. The miracles of faith and believe that would manifest many a dreams.

I am much grateful for my journey with Christ Jesus and his blessings. Much love for Christ Jesus as he loved us first.

1 John 4:19 esv
"We love because he first loved us."

Much Blessings with Love
& Lots of Miracles

Shalom,
Kyrra
a child of God …

1 John 3:1 niv
See what great love the Father has lavished on us, that we should be called children of God! And that is what we are! The reason the world does not know us is that it did not know him.

About the Book

A spiritual experience, thought provoking, transformational, informative, timeless & enduring to all believers …

Matthew 14:25-33nkjv

In the fourth watch of the night Jesus went to them, walking on the sea. The disciples saw him walking on the sea, were troubled with fear.

Disciples: It is a ghost!

Jesus: Be of good cheer! It is I. Do not be afraid.

Peter: Lord! If it is You, command me to walk to you on the water.

Jesus: Walk!

And when Peter had come down out of the boat, he walked on the water to go to Jesus. But when he saw that the wind was boisterous he was afraid, beginning to sink he cried out.

Peter: Lord, save me!

And immediately Jesus stretched out his hand and caught him.

Jesus: O you of little faith, why did you doubt?

And when they got into the boat, the wind ceased.

Then those who were in the boat came and worshiped him.

Everyone: Truly! You are the Son of God!

About the Author

Kyrra delights herself as a simpleton, attributing her credentials to the miracle of Christ Jesus. A single mum, baptized on a beautiful Easter day, loves her amazing daughter, who studies Pastoral Care Leadership, away at Hillsong College Sydney. Previous book published, Our Essence within Contemporary Haiku and she considers her works objet d'art. At this moment of time, Kyrra lives in Singapore.